Introduction

Welcome to Japanese Reading Practice for Beginners: 60 Guided Stories. I'm Haruki Yamamoto, and it's a true pleasure to accompany you on this journey into Japanese language and culture. If you're here, you've likely felt the same pull that I did—a curiosity about Japanese that goes beyond words on a page and into a world filled with unique expressions, values, and stories. My hope is that through this book, you'll feel that connection growing with each story and deepen your appreciation for the language in ways that feel meaningful and personal.

For me, Japanese has always been more than just a means of communication; it's a bridge to a rich and layered culture. Growing up, I was surrounded by little glimpses of this world, whether in conversations at home or the small details of family traditions. But it was only later in life that I felt a deeper urge to reconnect with the language, to truly immerse myself in the words and sounds that had been in the background of my life. As I began to study, I uncovered a beauty I hadn't fully seen before—the quiet wisdom embedded in the simplest phrases, the joy of expressions that capture feelings uniquely Japanese, and the rhythms of daily life woven into the words themselves. Language is powerful because it connects us not only to each other, but to the traditions, values, and emotions that define a culture.

I created this book with one core goal: to make learning Japanese as engaging, accessible, and joyful as possible. I still remember the mix of excitement and challenge I felt when I was starting out. The thrill of recognizing a kanji character or understanding a sentence is deeply satisfying, but there's also the occasional feeling of being overwhelmed by a language that can feel so different. This book is designed to ease those early steps by offering structured support, like helpful vocabulary lists, pronunciation aids, and line-by-line explanations. I wanted to make sure that each story feels like a manageable, enjoyable step forward, so that you're able to focus on absorbing the language naturally without feeling rushed or pressured.

In the first part of this book, you'll find a foundational vocabulary list and kanji chart to help ground your learning. These are words and characters that will appear frequently in Japanese, building up a core that you can rely on as you progress. By familiarizing yourself with these essentials, you'll be able to approach each story with confidence, recognizing key words and beginning to understand the flow of Japanese sentences. Learning vocabulary can sometimes feel like a chore, but I encourage you to see it as a way to bring the stories to life in your mind, as if you're piecing together a puzzle that reveals something new and exciting.

Each of the 60 stories in this book is crafted with beginners in mind, offering a glimpse into everyday moments and interactions in Japan. These aren't just isolated sentences or drills; they're small stories, rich with context, that reflect real aspects of Japanese life. You'll read about characters traveling, making friends, navigating daily routines, and experiencing emotions that are universally relatable. Through these stories, I hope you'll gain not only language skills, but also a sense of the cultural nuances that make Japanese so distinct and beautiful. Japanese expressions often capture ideas and emotions in ways that feel fresh and unique; by exploring these through the stories, you'll gradually develop an intuition for the culture itself, deepening your understanding far beyond vocabulary and grammar.

In addition to reading practice, I've included cultural insights throughout the book. Learning Japanese is about more than just memorizing words or phrases; it's about appreciating the values and perspectives that lie beneath the language. Japan's culture has a remarkable respect for nature, simplicity, and harmony, which is often reflected in the language. Even small expressions can carry a sense of humility, mindfulness, or warmth. By sharing these cultural notes, I hope to offer a richer experience that goes beyond the mechanics of learning, helping you connect with the essence of Japanese thinking and ways of life.

The book also includes comprehension questions to gently test your understanding and deepen your engagement with each story. These questions are designed not only to reinforce what you've read, but to help you reflect on the nuances of the language. You'll also find line-by-line breakdowns of each story, where we examine the sentence structure, grammar points, and vocabulary in detail. My goal here is to make Japanese feel approachable and transparent, so that even unfamiliar phrases start to feel intuitive and accessible. Learning the "why" behind the language can make all the difference, giving you the tools to move beyond memorization and truly engage with Japanese on your own terms.

And then, there's romaji—a tool to simplify pronunciation for beginners. Although it's best to transition to kana and kanji as you progress, romaji offers a helpful starting point, giving you a sense of the sounds and rhythms of Japanese speech. You'll find that as you practice, the flow of Japanese words and sentences will start to feel natural, almost like a melody. Pronunciation, rhythm, and flow are all integral parts of truly connecting with a language, and I hope that romaji serves as a useful bridge as you start to develop a feel for these elements.

Whether you're learning Japanese to connect with family, to travel, to explore a new culture, or simply to challenge yourself, this book is here to support you. Language learning is often seen as a path to mastery, but it's equally a journey of discovery, each new word and sentence broadening your perspective. My hope is that through these 60 stories, you'll find joy in each step of that journey, gaining both knowledge and confidence with every page.

So, as we set off together, remember that language learning is as much about curiosity as it is about effort. Embrace the challenges, celebrate the little victories, and let each story bring you closer to the heart of Japanese culture. Thank you for allowing me to be a part of your journey. I hope this book becomes a companion that you return to again and again, each time discovering something new and meaningful.

Enjoy your reading, and let's begin this adventure together.

Haruki Yamamoto

How to Get the Most Out of This Book

Welcome to *Japanese Reading Practice for Beginners: 60 Guided Stories*! This book was designed with one main goal: to make learning Japanese engaging, accessible, and straightforward. With 60 stories crafted to introduce you to real-life Japanese language and interactions, each page brings you closer to the heart of the language with support at every step. Here are some tips to help you dive right in and get the most out of your experience.

1. Dive Right In!

This book is meant to be an immersive experience, so don't worry about "preparing" or learning vocabulary ahead of time. Every story has built-in tools to guide you as you go. Each story introduces you to new vocabulary naturally and offers support in understanding grammar and sentence structure without overwhelming you.

Approach to Reading:

- **Read the Story Through First**: Let yourself read through each story naturally, noticing the context and main idea without overthinking any unknown words. Take it all in!

- **Use the Furigana and Romaji as Needed**: Furigana (small hiragana above kanji) is provided in each story to help with pronunciation. Romaji and English translations are also there if you need an extra nudge.

2. Check Comprehension with Each Story

Each story includes a comprehension question to help you test your understanding. Use these questions to see how much you grasped from the story and to highlight any areas that you may want to review.

Tips for Comprehension Questions:

- **Answer in Japanese When Possible**: Even if it's a short phrase or simple response, answering in Japanese helps reinforce what you've learned.

- **Revisit the Story for Clarity**: If you're unsure of an answer, read the relevant lines again and make use of the line-by-line breakdown if you need extra support.

3. Use the Line-by-Line Breakdown to Deepen Your Understanding

After each story, you'll find a detailed breakdown of every line, including vocabulary explanations, grammar notes, and translations. This breakdown is here to clarify any areas that might have been confusing in your first read-through.

How to Use the Breakdown:

- **Study Each Sentence Separately**: Read the Japanese sentence, then its romaji, and finally its English translation to gain a full understanding.

- **Focus on Vocabulary and Grammar**: Notice how vocabulary is used in context and pay attention to the grammar structures. This will help you recognize similar structures in other stories.

- **Reread with New Insights**: Once you feel comfortable with the breakdown, go back to the original story. You'll be surprised at how much more you understand!

4. Practice Pronunciation with Furigana and Romaji

Every kanji in the main story is accompanied by furigana to support your pronunciation. Romaji is also provided as an optional guide to make sure you can confidently pronounce each sentence. While romaji can be helpful, try to lean on the furigana to build familiarity with Japanese characters over time.

Suggestions for Practice:

- **Read Aloud**: Reading the story out loud, focusing on the furigana or romaji, helps you get a feel for the rhythm of Japanese and builds confidence in pronunciation.

- **Gradually Wean Off Romaji**: Romaji is a helpful starting point, but as you get more comfortable, try focusing on the Japanese characters and furigana instead.

5. Review and Reinforce Key Vocabulary and Kanji

At the beginning of the book, you'll find a vocabulary and kanji list with words that appear frequently in the stories. Refer back to this list whenever you want a quick reminder, or set aside time to review it as you progress.

How to Use Vocabulary for Maximum Benefit:

- **Spot Words in Stories**: Look for these key words in each story, which will make it easier to absorb them through repetition.

- **Review After Every Few Stories**: A quick review of the vocabulary and kanji every few stories can reinforce your learning and build confidence.

6. Find Your Own Pace

This book is designed to be flexible—whether you're a casual learner or diving into Japanese with focused intent, you can set your own rhythm. Some stories may feel easy, while others may require more focus, and that's okay. The goal is progress, not perfection.

Encouragement for a Balanced Approach:

- **Celebrate Small Wins**: Each story you complete is a step forward. Recognize your progress and stay positive!

- **Take Breaks When Needed**: Don't rush or worry if you need to reread a story or revisit the breakdown. Consistency is key, and each review will help deepen your understanding.

By following these tips, you'll be well-prepared to make steady progress through each story and develop a solid foundation in Japanese reading comprehension. This book is here to support you every step of the way, with tools designed to make learning Japanese enjoyable, enriching, and straightforward. Dive in, explore each story, and find joy in the journey of learning Japanese!

Story 1: はじめての日本 (First Time in Japan)

Story in Japanese

ジョンさんはアメリカ人です。初めて日本に来ました。空港で友達に会います。友達は「ようこそ、日本へ！」と言います。

Comprehension Question

- ジョンさんはどこで友達に会いますか？
  (Where does John meet his friend?)

Story with Line-by-Line Breakdown

ジョンさんはアメリカ人です。

- **Japanese:** ジョンさんはアメリカ人です。

- **Romaji:** Jon-san wa Amerika-jin desu.

- **English:** John is an American.

Grammar and Vocabulary:

- ジョンさん **(Jon-san):** John's name with honorific "san" used for politeness.

- アメリカ人 **(Amerika-jin):** American person; "人" means "person."

- です **(desu):** a polite ending used for statements.

初めて日本に来ました。

- **Japanese:** 初めて日本に来ました。

- **Romaji:** Hajimete Nihon ni kimashita.

- **English:** He came to Japan for the first time.

Grammar and Vocabulary:

- 初めて **(hajimete):** first time.

- 日本 **(Nihon):** Japan.

- に **(ni):** indicates direction or destination.

- 来ました **(kimashita):** past form of "kuru" (to come); polite past tense.

空港で友達に会います。

- **Japanese:** 空港で友達に会います。

- **Romaji:** Kuukou de tomodachi ni aimasu.

- **English:** He meets a friend at the airport.

Grammar and Vocabulary:

- 空港 **(kuukou):** airport.

- で **(de):** indicates the location where an action takes place.

- 友達 **(tomodachi):** friend.

- に **(ni):** indicates the indirect object (whom he meets).

- 会います **(aimasu):** to meet.

友達は「ようこそ、日本へ！」と言います。

- **Japanese:** 友達は「ようこそ、日本へ！」と言います。

- **Romaji:** Tomodachi wa "Youkoso, Nihon e!" to iimasu.

- **English:** The friend says, "Welcome to Japan!"

Grammar and Vocabulary:

- ようこそ **(youkoso):** welcome.

- 日本へ **(Nihon e):** to Japan; "へ" indicates direction.

- と言います **(to iimasu):** says (indirect quote marker "と" + "言います" to say).

Story 2: ホテルへ行く (Going to the Hotel)

Story in Japanese

ジョンさんはバスでホテルに行きます。バスの中はとても静かです。ジョンさんは窓から町を見ます。

Comprehension Question

- ジョンさんは何でホテルに行きますか？
  (How does John go to the hotel?)

Story with Line-by-Line Breakdown

ジョンさんはバスでホテルに行きます。

- **Japanese:** ジョンさんはバスでホテルに行きます。

- **Romaji:** Jon-san wa basu de hoteru ni ikimasu.

- **English:** John goes to the hotel by bus.

Grammar and Vocabulary:

- バス **(basu):** bus.

- で **(de):** indicates the means by which something is done (by bus).

- ホテル **(hoteru):** hotel.

- に **(ni):** indicates destination.

- 行きます **(ikimasu):** to go; polite form.

バスの中はとても静かです。

- **Japanese:** バスの中はとても静かです。

- **Romaji:** Basu no naka wa totemo shizuka desu.

- **English:** Inside the bus, it is very quiet.

Grammar and Vocabulary:

- バスの中 **(basu no naka):** inside the bus.

- は **(wa):** topic marker.

- とても **(totemo):** very.

- 静か **(shizuka):** quiet; "na" adjective.

- です **(desu):** polite sentence ending.

ジョンさんは窓から町を見ます。

- **Japanese:** ジョンさんは窓から町を見ます。

- **Romaji:** Jon-san wa mado kara machi o mimasu.

- **English:** John looks at the town from the window.

Grammar and Vocabulary:

- 窓 **(mado):** window.

- から **(kara):** from; indicates starting point.

- 町 **(machi):** town.

- を **(o):** object marker.

- 見ます **(mimasu):** to look at; polite form.

Story 3: 朝ごはんを食べる (Eating Breakfast)

Story in Japanese

朝、ジョンさんはホテルで朝ごはんを食べます。ご飯
とみそ汁と魚です。「とてもおいしいです！」と
ジョンさんは言います。

Comprehension Question

- ジョンさんは朝ごはんに何を食べますか？
  (What does John eat for breakfast?)

Story with Line-by-Line Breakdown

朝、ジョンさんはホテルで朝ごはんを食べます。

- **Japanese:** 朝、ジョンさんはホテルで朝ごはんを食べます。

- **Romaji:** Asa, Jon-san wa hoteru de asagohan o tabemasu.

- **English:** In the morning, John eats breakfast at the hotel.

Grammar and Vocabulary:

- 朝 **(asa):** morning.

- ホテルで **(hoteru de):** at the hotel; "で" indicates location.

- 朝ごはん **(asagohan):** breakfast.

- を **(o):** object marker.

- 食べます **(tabemasu):** to eat; polite form.

ご飯とみそ汁と魚です。

- **Japanese:** ご飯とみそ汁と魚です。

- **Romaji:** Gohan to misoshiru to sakana desu.

- **English:** It's rice, miso soup, and fish.

Grammar and Vocabulary:

- ご飯 **(gohan):** rice; also used for "meal."

- みそ汁 **(misoshiru):** miso soup.

- 魚 **(sakana):** fish.

- です **(desu):** polite sentence ending.

「とてもおいしいです！」とジョンさんは言います。

- **Japanese:** 「とてもおいしいです！」とジョンさんは言います。

- **Romaji:** "Totemo oishii desu!" to Jon-san wa iimasu.

- **English:** "It's very delicious!" says John.

Grammar and Vocabulary:

- とても **(totemo):** very.

- おいしい **(oishii):** delicious; "i" adjective.

- と言います **(to iimasu):** says (quotation marker "と" + "言います" to say).

Story 4: 東京タワーを見に行く (Going to See Tokyo Tower)

Story in Japanese

ジョンさんは東京タワーに行きます。高いタワーで
す。上からの景色はきれいです。

Comprehension Question

- ジョンさんはどこに行きますか？
  (Where does John go?)

Story with Line-by-Line Breakdown

ジョンさんは東京タワーに行きます。

- **Japanese:** ジョンさんは東京タワーに行きます。

- **Romaji:** Jon-san wa Toukyou tawaa ni ikimasu.

- **English:** John goes to Tokyo Tower.

Grammar and Vocabulary:

- 東京タワー **(Toukyou tawaa):** Tokyo Tower.

- に **(ni):** indicates the destination.

- 行きます **(ikimasu):** to go; polite form.

高いタワーです。

- **Japanese:** 高いタワーです。

- **Romaji:** Takai tawaa desu.

- **English:** It is a tall tower.

Grammar and Vocabulary:

- 高い **(takai):** tall; "i" adjective.

- タワー **(tawaa):** tower.

- です **(desu):** polite sentence ending.

上からの景色はきれいです。

- **Japanese:** 上からの景色はきれいです。

- **Romaji:** Ue kara no keshiki wa kirei desu.

- **English:** The view from the top is beautiful.

Grammar and Vocabulary:

- 上から **(ue kara):** from the top.

- 景色 **(keshiki):** view/scenery.

- は **(wa):** topic marker.

- きれい **(kirei):** beautiful; "na" adjective.

- です **(desu):** polite sentence ending.

Story 5: 電車に乗る (Riding the Train)

Story in Japanese

ジョンさんは電車に乗ります。日本の電車は速いです。

駅で降ります。

Comprehension Question

- ジョンさんはどこで降りますか？
  (Where does John get off?)

Story with Line-by-Line Breakdown

ジョンさんは電車に乗ります。

- **Japanese:** ジョンさんは電車に乗ります。

- **Romaji:** Jon-san wa densha ni norimasu.

- **English:** John rides the train.

Grammar and Vocabulary:

- 電車 **(densha):** train.

- に **(ni):** indicates the object of riding.

- 乗ります **(norimasu):** to ride; polite form.

日本の電車は速いです。

- **Japanese:** 日本の電車は速いです。

- **Romaji:** Nihon no densha wa hayai desu.

- **English:** Japanese trains are fast.

Grammar and Vocabulary:

- 日本の電車 **(Nihon no densha):** Japanese train; "の" indicates possession.

- 速い **(hayai):** fast; "i" adjective.

- です **(desu):** polite sentence ending.

駅で降ります。

- **Japanese:** 駅で降ります。

- **Romaji:** Eki de orimasu.

- **English:** He gets off at the station.

Grammar and Vocabulary:

- 駅 **(eki):** station.

- で **(de):** indicates location of the action.

- 降ります **(orimasu):** to get off; polite form.

Story 6: 公園で休む (Resting in the Park)

Story in Japanese

ジョンさんは公園で休みます。ベンチに座って、空を見ます。天気は晴れです。

Comprehension Question

- ジョンさんは公園で何をしますか？
  (What does John do in the park?)

Story with Line-by-Line Breakdown

ジョンさんは公園で休みます。

- **Japanese:** ジョンさんは公園で休みます。

- **Romaji:** Jon-san wa kouen de yasumimasu.

- **English:** John rests in the park.

Grammar and Vocabulary:

- 公園 **(kouen):** park.

- で **(de):** indicates location where the action takes place.

- 休みます **(yasumimasu):** to rest; polite form.

ベンチに座って、空を見ます。

- **Japanese:** ベンチに座って、空を見ます。

- **Romaji:** Benchi ni suwatte, sora o mimasu.

- **English:** He sits on a bench and looks at the sky.

Grammar and Vocabulary:

- ベンチ **(benchi):** bench.

- に **(ni):** indicates direction (to the bench).

- 座って **(suwatte):** "te" form of "suwaru" (to sit); used for sequential actions.

- 空 **(sora):** sky.

- を **(o):** object marker.

- 見ます **(mimasu):** to look; polite form.

天気は晴れです。

- **Japanese:** 天気は晴れです。

- **Romaji:** Tenki wa hare desu.

- **English:** The weather is clear.

Grammar and Vocabulary:

- 天気 **(tenki):** weather.

- は **(wa):** topic marker.

- 晴れ **(hare):** clear (weather).

- です **(desu):** polite sentence ending.

Story 7: お昼ごはんを買う (Buying Lunch)

Story in Japanese

ジョンさんはコンビニでお昼ごはんを買います。おにぎりとお茶です。公園で食べます。

Comprehension Question

- ジョンさんはどこでお昼ごはんを買いますか？
  (Where does John buy his lunch?)

Story with Line-by-Line Breakdown

ジョンさんはコンビニでお昼ごはんを買います。

- **Japanese:** ジョンさんはコンビニでお昼ごはんを買います。

- **Romaji:** Jon-san wa konbini de ohirugohan o kaimasu.

- **English:** John buys lunch at the convenience store.

Grammar and Vocabulary:

- コンビニ **(konbini):** convenience store.

- で **(de):** indicates the location of the action.

- お昼ごはん **(ohirugohan):** lunch.

- を **(o):** object marker.

- 買います **(kaimasu):** to buy; polite form.

おにぎりとお茶です。

- **Japanese:** おにぎりとお茶です。

- **Romaji:** Onigiri to ocha desu.

- **English:** It's rice balls and tea.

Grammar and Vocabulary:

- おにぎり **(onigiri):** rice balls.

- お茶 **(ocha):** tea.

- です **(desu):** polite sentence ending.

公園で食べます。

- **Japanese:** 公園で食べます。

- **Romaji:** Kouen de tabemasu.

- **English:** He eats in the park.

Grammar and Vocabulary:

- 公園 **(kouen):** park.

- で **(de):** indicates the location of the action.

- 食べます **(tabemasu):** to eat; polite form.

Story 8: 神社を訪ねる (Visiting a Shrine)

Story in Japanese

ジョンさんは神社に行きます。大きい鳥居がありま

す。写真を撮ります。

Comprehension Question

- ジョンさんは神社で何をしますか？
  (What does John do at the shrine?)

Story with Line-by-Line Breakdown

ジョンさんは神社に行きます。

- **Japanese:** ジョンさんは神社に行きます。

- **Romaji:** Jon-san wa jinja ni ikimasu.

- **English:** John goes to the shrine.

Grammar and Vocabulary:

- 神社 **(jinja):** shrine.

- に **(ni):** indicates the destination.

- 行きます **(ikimasu):** to go; polite form.

大きい鳥居があります。

- **Japanese:** 大きい鳥居があります。

- **Romaji:** Ookii torii ga arimasu.

- **English:** There is a large torii gate.

Grammar and Vocabulary:

- 大きい **(ookii):** big; "i" adjective.

- 鳥居 **(torii):** traditional Japanese gate found at the entrance of a shrine.

- が **(ga):** subject marker.

- あります **(arimasu):** to exist; used for non-living things.

写真を撮ります。

- **Japanese:** 写真を撮ります。

- **Romaji:** Shashin o torimasu.

- **English:** He takes a picture.

Grammar and Vocabulary:

- 写真 **(shashin):** picture.

- を **(o):** object marker.

- 撮ります **(torimasu):** to take (a photo); polite form.

Story 9: お土産を買う (Buying Souvenirs)

Story in Japanese

ジョンさんは店でお土産を買います。友達にあげます。きれいな扇子です。

Comprehension Question

- ジョンさんはお土産を誰にあげますか？
  (Who does John give the souvenir to?)

Story with Line-by-Line Breakdown

ジョンさんは店でお土産を買います。

- **Japanese:** ジョンさんは店でお土産を買います。

- **Romaji:** Jon-san wa mise de omiyage o kaimasu.

- **English:** John buys a souvenir at the store.

Grammar and Vocabulary:

- 店 **(mise):** store.

- で **(de):** indicates the location of the action.

- お土産 **(omiyage):** souvenir.

- を **(o):** object marker.

- 買います **(kaimasu):** to buy; polite form.

友達にあげます。

- **Japanese:** 友達にあげます。

- **Romaji:** Tomodachi ni agemasu.

- **English:** He gives it to his friend.

Grammar and Vocabulary:

- 友達 **(tomodachi):** friend.

- に **(ni):** indicates the recipient.

- あげます **(agemasu):** to give; polite form.

きれいな扇子です。

- **Japanese:** きれいな扇子です。

- **Romaji:** Kirei na sensu desu.

- **English:** It's a beautiful fan.

Grammar and Vocabulary:

- きれい **(kirei):** beautiful; "na" adjective.

- 扇子 **(sensu):** fan.

- です **(desu):** polite sentence ending.

Story 10: 日本語を話す (Speaking Japanese)

Story in Japanese

ジョンさんは店員さんに日本語で話します。「これを
ください」と言います。店員さんは「ありがとうござ
います」と言います。

Comprehension Question

- ジョンさんは何語で店員さんに話しますか？
  (What language does John use to speak to the store clerk?)

Story with Line-by-Line Breakdown

ジョンさんは店員さんに日本語で話します。

- **Japanese:** ジョンさんは店員さんに日本語で話します。

- **Romaji:** Jon-san wa ten'in-san ni nihongo de hanashimasu.

- **English:** John speaks to the store clerk in Japanese.

Grammar and Vocabulary:

- 店員さん **(ten'in-san):** store clerk; "さん" is an honorific for politeness.

- に **(ni):** indicates the person he is speaking to.

- 日本語で **(nihongo de):** in Japanese; "で" indicates the language or means.

- 話します **(hanashimasu):** to speak; polite form.

「これをください」と言います。

- **Japanese:** 「これをください」と言います。

- **Romaji:** "Kore o kudasai" to iimasu.

- **English:** He says, "Please give me this."

Grammar and Vocabulary:

- これ **(kore):** this (referring to something near the speaker).

- を **(o):** object marker.

- ください **(kudasai):** please give (polite request).

- と言います **(to iimasu):** to say; indirect quote marker "と" + "言います."

店員さんは「ありがとうございます」と言います。

- **Japanese:** 店員さんは「ありがとうございます」と言います。

- **Romaji:** Ten'in-san wa "arigatou gozaimasu" to iimasu.

- **English:** The store clerk says, "Thank you very much."

Grammar and Vocabulary:

- ありがとうございます **(arigatou gozaimasu):** thank you very much (polite form).

- と言います **(to iimasu):** to say; indirect quote marker "と" + "言います."

Story 11: 美術館に行く (Going to the Art Museum)

Story in Japanese

ジョンさんは美術館に行きます。日本の絵を見ます。

とても興味深いです。

Comprehension Question

- ジョンさんは美術館で何を見ますか？
  (What does John see at the art museum?)

Story with Line-by-Line Breakdown

ジョンさんは美術館に行きます。

- **Japanese:** ジョンさんは美術館に行きます。

- **Romaji:** Jon-san wa bijutsukan ni ikimasu.

- **English:** John goes to the art museum.

Grammar and Vocabulary:

- 美術館 **(bijutsukan):** art museum.

- に **(ni):** indicates the destination.

- 行きます **(ikimasu):** to go; polite form.

日本の絵を見ます。

- **Japanese:** 日本の絵を見ます。

- **Romaji:** Nihon no e o mimasu.

- **English:** He looks at Japanese paintings.

Grammar and Vocabulary:

- 日本の絵 **(Nihon no e):** Japanese paintings; "の" indicates possession (Japanese).

- を **(o):** object marker.

- 見ます **(mimasu):** to look at; polite form.

とても興味深いです。

- **Japanese:** とても興味深いです。

- **Romaji:** Totemo kyoumibukai desu.

- **English:** It's very interesting.

Grammar and Vocabulary:

- とても **(totemo):** very.

- 興味深い **(kyoumibukai):** interesting; "i" adjective.

- です **(desu):** polite sentence ending.

Story 12: レストランで晩ごはん (Dinner at a Restaurant)

Story in Japanese

夜、ジョンさんはレストランで晩ごはんを食べます。

寿司や天ぷらがあります。日本酒も飲みます。

Comprehension Question

- ジョンさんは晩ごはんに何を食べますか？
  (What does John eat for dinner?)

Story with Line-by-Line Breakdown

夜、ジョンさんはレストランで晩ごはんを食べます。

- **Japanese:** 夜、ジョンさんはレストランで晩ごはんを食べます。

- **Romaji:** Yoru, Jon-san wa resutoran de bangohan o tabemasu.

- **English:** In the evening, John eats dinner at a restaurant.

Grammar and Vocabulary:

- 夜 **(yoru):** evening/night.

- レストランで **(resutoran de):** at the restaurant; "で" indicates location.

- 晩ごはん **(bangohan):** dinner.

- を **(o):** object marker.

- 食べます **(tabemasu):** to eat; polite form.

寿司や天ぷらがあります。

- **Japanese:** 寿司や天ぷらがあります。

- **Romaji:** Sushi ya tenpura ga arimasu.

- **English:** There is sushi and tempura.

Grammar and Vocabulary:

- 寿司 **(sushi):** sushi.

- 天ぷら **(tenpura):** tempura.

- や **(ya):** and (used to list a few items, not an exhaustive list).

- あります **(arimasu):** to exist; used for non-living things.

日本酒も飲みます。

- **Japanese:** 日本酒も飲みます。

- **Romaji:** Nihonshu mo nomimasu.

- **English:** He also drinks sake.

Grammar and Vocabulary:

- 日本酒 **(nihonshu):** sake (Japanese rice wine).

- も **(mo):** also; adds information.

- 飲みます **(nomimasu):** to drink; polite form.

Story 13: ホテルに帰る (Returning to the Hotel)

Story in Japanese

ジョンさんはタクシーでホテルに帰ります。運転手さんは親切です。

Comprehension Question

- ジョンさんはどうやってホテルに帰りますか？
  (How does John return to the hotel?)

Story with Line-by-Line Breakdown

ジョンさんはタクシーでホテルに帰ります。

- **Japanese:** ジョンさんはタクシーでホテルに帰ります。

- **Romaji:** Jon-san wa takushii de hoteru ni kaerimasu.

- **English:** John returns to the hotel by taxi.

Grammar and Vocabulary:

- タクシー **(takushii):** taxi.

- で **(de):** indicates the means of transportation.

- ホテル **(hoteru):** hotel.

- に **(ni):** indicates destination.

- 帰ります **(kaerimasu):** to return; polite form.

運転手さんは親切です。

- **Japanese:** 運転手さんは親切です。

- **Romaji:** Untenshu-san wa shinsetsu desu.

- **English:** The driver is kind.

Grammar and Vocabulary:

- 運転手さん **(untenshu-san):** driver; "さん" is an honorific.

- 親切 **(shinsetsu):** kind; "na" adjective.

- です **(desu):** polite sentence ending.

Story 14: 温泉に入る (Entering a Hot Spring)

Story in Japanese

次（つぎ）の日（ひ）、ジョンさんは温泉（おんせん）に行（い）きます。熱（あつ）いお湯（ゆ）に入（はい）ります。とても気持（きも）ちがいいです。

Comprehension Question

- ジョンさんは温泉で何をしますか？
  (What does John do at the hot spring?)

Story with Line-by-Line Breakdown

次の日、ジョンさんは温泉に行きます。

- **Japanese:** 次の日、ジョンさんは温泉に行きます。

- **Romaji:** Tsugi no hi, Jon-san wa onsen ni ikimasu.

- **English:** The next day, John goes to the hot spring.

Grammar and Vocabulary:

- 次の日 **(tsugi no hi):** the next day.

- 温泉 **(onsen):** hot spring.

- に **(ni):** indicates the destination.

- 行きます **(ikimasu):** to go; polite form.

熱いお湯に入ります。

- **Japanese:** 熱いお湯に入ります。

- **Romaji:** Atsui oyu ni hairimasu.

- **English:** He enters the hot water.

Grammar and Vocabulary:

- 熱い **(atsui):** hot (for objects/liquids).

- お湯 **(oyu):** hot water.

- に **(ni):** indicates where he is entering.

- 入ります **(hairimasu):** to enter; polite form.

とても気持ちがいいです。

- **Japanese:** とても気持ちがいいです。

- **Romaji:** Totemo kimochi ga ii desu.

- **English:** It feels very good.

Grammar and Vocabulary:

- とても **(totemo):** very.

- 気持ちがいい **(kimochi ga ii):** feels good.

- です **(desu):** polite sentence ending.

Story 15: 山に登る (Climbing a Mountain)

JOHN
American

Story in Japanese

ジョンさんは山に登ります。少し疲れますが、景色は最高です。

Comprehension Question

- ジョンさんは山で何を感じますか？
  (What does John feel on the mountain?)

Story with Line-by-Line Breakdown

ジョンさんは山に登ります。

- **Japanese:** ジョンさんは山に登ります。

- **Romaji:** Jon-san wa yama ni noborimasu.

- **English:** John climbs the mountain.

Grammar and Vocabulary:

- 山 **(yama):** mountain.

- に **(ni):** indicates the direction or goal.

- 登ります **(noborimasu):** to climb; polite form.

少し疲れますが、景色は最高です。

- **Japanese:** 少し疲れますが、景色は最高です。

- **Romaji:** Sukoshi tsukaremasu ga, keshiki wa saikou desu.

- **English:** He gets a little tired, but the view is amazing.

Grammar and Vocabulary:

- 少し **(sukoshi):** a little.

- 疲れます **(tsukaremasu):** to get tired; polite form.

- が **(ga):** but (used to contrast phrases).

- 景色 **(keshiki):** scenery/view.

- 最高 **(saikou):** best/amazing.

- です **(desu):** polite sentence ending.

Story 16: 祭りを見る (Watching the Festival)

Story in Japanese

ジョンさんは祭りを見ます。たくさんの人がいます。

屋台で食べ物を買います。

Comprehension Question

- ジョンさんはどこで食べ物を買いますか？
  (Where does John buy food?)

Story with Line-by-Line Breakdown

ジョンさんは祭りを見ます。

- **Japanese:** ジョンさんは祭りを見ます。

- **Romaji:** Jon-san wa matsuri o mimasu.

- **English:** John watches the festival.

Grammar and Vocabulary:

- 祭り **(matsuri):** festival.

- を **(o):** object marker.

- 見ます **(mimasu):** to watch/see; polite form.

たくさんの人がいます。

- **Japanese:** たくさんの人がいます。

- **Romaji:** Takusan no hito ga imasu.

- **English:** There are many people.

Grammar and Vocabulary:

- たくさんの **(takusan no):** many/lots of.

- 人 **(hito):** people.

- が **(ga):** subject marker.

- います **(imasu):** to exist; used for living beings.

屋台で食べ物を買います。

- **Japanese:** 屋台で食べ物を買います。

- **Romaji:** Yatai de tabemono o kaimasu.

- **English:** He buys food at a food stall.

Grammar and Vocabulary:

- 屋台 **(yatai):** food stall.

- で **(de):** indicates location.

- 食べ物 **(tabemono):** food.

- を **(o):** object marker.

- 買います **(kaimasu):** to buy; polite form.

Story 17: 花見をする (Cherry Blossom Viewing)

Story in Japanese

春です。ジョンさんは公園で花見をします。桜の花
<ruby>春<rt>はる</rt></ruby>です。<ruby>ジョン<rt>じょん</rt></ruby>さんは<ruby>公園<rt>こうえん</rt></ruby>で<ruby>花見<rt>はなみ</rt></ruby>をします。<ruby>桜<rt>さくら</rt></ruby>の<ruby>花<rt>はな</rt></ruby>

がきれいです。

Comprehension Question

- ジョンさんはどこで花見をしますか？
  (Where does John do cherry blossom viewing?)

Story with Line-by-Line Breakdown

春です。

- **Japanese:** 春です。

- **Romaji:** Haru desu.

- **English:** It's spring.

Grammar and Vocabulary:

- 春 **(haru):** spring.

- です **(desu):** polite sentence ending.

ジョンさんは公園で花見をします。

- **Japanese:** ジョンさんは公園で花見をします。

- **Romaji:** Jon-san wa kouen de hanami o shimasu.

- **English:** John does cherry blossom viewing at the park.

Grammar and Vocabulary:

- 公園 **(kouen):** park.

- で **(de):** indicates location.

- 花見 **(hanami):** cherry blossom viewing.

- を **(o):** object marker.

- します **(shimasu):** to do; polite form.

桜の花がきれいです。

- **Japanese:** 桜の花がきれいです。

- **Romaji:** Sakura no hana ga kirei desu.

- **English:** The cherry blossoms are beautiful.

Grammar and Vocabulary:

- 桜 **(sakura):** cherry blossom.

- 花 **(hana):** flower.

- が **(ga):** subject marker.

- きれい **(kirei):** beautiful; "na" adjective.

- です **(desu):** polite sentence ending.

Story 18: 動物園に行く (Going to the Zoo)

Story in Japanese

ジョンさんは動物園に行きます。パンダや象を見ます。子供たちは楽しそうです。

Comprehension Question

- ジョンさんは動物園で何を見ますか？
  (What does John see at the zoo?)

Story with Line-by-Line Breakdown

ジョンさんは動物園に行きます。

- **Japanese:** ジョンさんは動物園に行きます。

- **Romaji:** Jon-san wa doubutsuen ni ikimasu.

- **English:** John goes to the zoo.

Grammar and Vocabulary:

- 動物園 **(doubutsuen):** zoo.

- に **(ni):** indicates the destination.

- 行きます **(ikimasu):** to go; polite form.

パンダや象を見ます。

- **Japanese:** パンダや象を見ます。

- **Romaji:** Panda ya zou o mimasu.

- **English:** He sees pandas and elephants.

Grammar and Vocabulary:

- パンダ **(panda):** panda.

- 象 **(zou):** elephant.

- や **(ya):** and (used to list examples, not exhaustive).

- を **(o):** object marker.

- 見ます **(mimasu):** to see; polite form.

子供たちは楽しそうです。

- **Japanese:** 子供たちは楽しそうです。

- **Romaji:** Kodomotachi wa tanoshisou desu.

- **English:** The children look happy.

Grammar and Vocabulary:

- 子供たち **(kodomotachi):** children.

- は **(wa):** topic marker.

- 楽しそう **(tanoshisou):** looks happy; "そう" adds a sense of appearance.

- です **(desu):** polite sentence ending.

Story 19: 帰りの準備 (Preparing to Return)

Story in Japanese

ジョンさんはホテルで荷物をまとめます。日本での思い出がたくさんあります。

Comprehension Question

- ジョンさんは何をまとめますか？
  (What does John pack up?)

Story with Line-by-Line Breakdown

ジョンさんはホテルで荷物をまとめます。

- **Japanese:** ジョンさんはホテルで荷物をまとめます。

- **Romaji:** Jon-san wa hoteru de nimotsu o matomemasu.

- **English:** John packs his luggage at the hotel.

Grammar and Vocabulary:

- ホテルで **(hoteru de):** at the hotel; "で" indicates location.

- 荷物 **(nimotsu):** luggage.

- を **(o):** object marker.

- まとめます **(matomemasu):** to pack/gather; polite form.

日本での思い出がたくさんあります。

- **Japanese:** 日本での思い出がたくさんあります。

- **Romaji:** Nihon de no omoide ga takusan arimasu.

- **English:** He has many memories of Japan.

Grammar and Vocabulary:

- 日本での **(Nihon de no):** of Japan (indicating location where memories were made).

- 思い出 **(omoide):** memories.

- が **(ga):** subject marker.

- たくさん **(takusan):** many/a lot.

- あります **(arimasu):** to have/exist; polite form (used for non-living things).

Story 20: 日本を出発する (Departing from Japan)

Story in Japanese

ジョンさんは飛行機で国に帰ります。「また日本に来たいです」と思います。

Comprehension Question

- ジョンさんは何で国に帰りますか？
  (How does John return to his country?)

Story with Line-by-Line Breakdown

ジョンさんは飛行機で国に帰ります。

- **Japanese:** ジョンさんは飛行機で国に帰ります。

- **Romaji:** Jon-san wa hikouki de kuni ni kaerimasu.

- **English:** John returns to his country by plane.

Grammar and Vocabulary:

- 飛行機 **(hikouki):** airplane.

- で **(de):** indicates the means of transportation.

- 国 **(kuni):** country.

- に **(ni):** indicates the destination.

- 帰ります **(kaerimasu):** to return; polite form.

「また日本に来たいです」と思います。

- **Japanese:** 「また日本に来たいです」と思います。

- **Romaji:** "Mata Nihon ni kitai desu" to omoimasu.

- **English:** He thinks, "I want to come to Japan again."

Grammar and Vocabulary:

- また **(mata):** again.

- 日本に来たい **(Nihon ni kitai):** want to come to Japan.

- です **(desu):** polite sentence ending.

- と思います **(to omoimasu):** to think; used to express thoughts or internal dialogue.

Story 21: お城を訪ねる (Visiting a Castle)

Story in Japanese

ジョンさんはお城に行きます。

大きくて古いお城です。

中にはたくさんの部屋があります。

ガイドさんが歴史を教えてくれます。

ジョンさんは写真をたくさん撮ります。

とても楽しい時間です。

Comprehension Question

- ジョンさんはお城で何をしますか？
  (What does John do at the castle?)

Story with Line-by-Line Breakdown

ジョンさんはお城に行きます。

- **Japanese:** ジョンさんはお城に行きます。

- **Romaji:** Jon-san wa oshiro ni ikimasu.

- **English:** John goes to the castle.

Grammar and Vocabulary:

- お城 **(oshiro):** castle; "お" is an honorific prefix for politeness.

- に **(ni):** indicates the destination.

- 行きます **(ikimasu):** to go; polite form.

大きくて古いお城です。

- **Japanese:** 大きくて古いお城です。

- **Romaji:** Ookikute furui oshiro desu.

- **English:** It's a big and old castle.

Grammar and Vocabulary:

- 大きくて **(ookikute):** big; "くて" is used to connect adjectives.

- 古い **(furui):** old; "i" adjective.

- です **(desu):** polite sentence ending.

中にはたくさんの部屋があります。

- **Japanese:** 中にはたくさんの部屋があります。

- **Romaji:** Naka ni wa takusan no heya ga arimasu.

- **English:** Inside, there are many rooms.

Grammar and Vocabulary:

- 中 **(naka):** inside.

- には **(ni wa):** combination of "ni" (indicating location) and "wa" (topic marker).

- たくさんの **(takusan no):** many/lots of.

- 部屋 **(heya):** rooms.

- が **(ga):** subject marker.

- あります **(arimasu):** to exist; used for non-living things.

ガイドさんが歴史を教えてくれます。

- **Japanese:** ガイドさんが歴史を教えてくれます。

- **Romaji:** Gaido-san ga rekishi o oshiete kuremasu.

- **English:** The guide teaches the history.

Grammar and Vocabulary:

- ガイドさん **(gaido-san):** guide; "さん" is an honorific for politeness.

- が **(ga):** subject marker.

- 歴史 **(rekishi):** history.

- を **(o):** object marker.

- 教えてくれます **(oshiete kuremasu):** to teach or explain (as a favor to the listener).

ジョンさんは写真をたくさん撮ります。

- **Japanese:** ジョンさんは写真をたくさん撮ります。

- **Romaji:** Jon-san wa shashin o takusan torimasu.

- **English:** John takes many pictures.

Grammar and Vocabulary:

- 写真 **(shashin):** picture/photo.

- を **(o):** object marker.

- たくさん **(takusan):** many/a lot.

- 撮ります **(torimasu):** to take (a photo); polite form.

とても楽しい時間です。

- **Japanese:** とても楽しい時間です。

- **Romaji:** Totemo tanoshii jikan desu.

- **English:** It's a very enjoyable time.

Grammar and Vocabulary:

- とても **(totemo):** very.

- 楽しい **(tanoshii):** enjoyable/fun; "i" adjective.

- 時間 **(jikan):** time.

- です **(desu):** polite sentence ending.

Story 22: 市場で買い物 (Shopping at the Market)

Story in Japanese

ジョンさんは市場に行きます。

新鮮な野菜や果物があります。

お店の人と話します。

日本語で値段を聞きます。

美味しそうなリンゴを買います。

買い物が楽しいです。

Comprehension Question

- ジョンさんは市場で何を買いますか？
  (What does John buy at the market?)

Story with Line-by-Line Breakdown

ジョンさんは市場に行きます。

- **Japanese:** ジョンさんは市場に行きます。

- **Romaji:** Jon-san wa ichiba ni ikimasu.

- **English:** John goes to the market.

Grammar and Vocabulary:

- 市場 **(ichiba):** market.

- に **(ni):** indicates the destination.

- 行きます **(ikimasu):** to go; polite form.

新鮮な野菜や果物があります。

- **Japanese:** 新鮮な野菜や果物があります。

- **Romaji:** Shinsen na yasai ya kudamono ga arimasu.

- **English:** There are fresh vegetables and fruits.

Grammar and Vocabulary:

- 新鮮な **(shinsen na):** fresh; "na" adjective.

- 野菜 **(yasai):** vegetables.

- 果物 **(kudamono):** fruits.

- や **(ya):** and (used for listing examples).

- が **(ga):** subject marker.

- あります **(arimasu):** to exist; used for non-living things.

お店の人と話します。

- **Japanese:** お店の人と話します。

- **Romaji:** Omise no hito to hanashimasu.

- **English:** He talks with the shopkeeper.

Grammar and Vocabulary:

- お店の人 **(omise no hito):** shopkeeper (literally "person of the shop").

- と **(to):** with (indicates the person he talks to).

- 話します **(hanashimasu):** to talk; polite form.

日本語で値段を聞きます。

- **Japanese:** 日本語で値段を聞きます。

- **Romaji:** Nihongo de nedan o kikimasu.

- **English:** He asks the price in Japanese.

Grammar and Vocabulary:

- 日本語で **(Nihongo de):** in Japanese.

- 値段 **(nedan):** price.

- を **(o):** object marker.

- 聞きます **(kikimasu):** to ask/listen; polite form.

美味しそうなリンゴを買います。

- **Japanese:** 美味しそうなリンゴを買います。

- **Romaji:** Oishisou na ringo o kaimasu.

- **English:** He buys a delicious-looking apple.

Grammar and Vocabulary:

- 美味しそうな **(oishisou na):** looks delicious.

- リンゴ **(ringo):** apple.

- を **(o):** object marker.

- 買います **(kaimasu):** to buy; polite form.

買い物が楽しいです。

- **Japanese:** 買い物が楽しいです。

- **Romaji:** Kaimono ga tanoshii desu.

- **English:** Shopping is fun.

Grammar and Vocabulary:

- 買い物 **(kaimono):** shopping.

- が **(ga):** subject marker.

- 楽しい **(tanoshii):** fun; "i" adjective.

- です **(desu):** polite sentence ending.

Story 23: 日本の家に泊まる (Staying at a Japanese House)

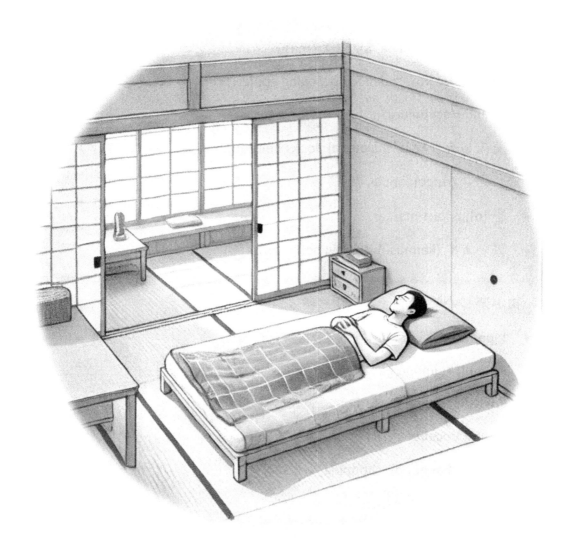

Story in Japanese

ジョンさんは友達の家に泊まります。

日本の家はとてもきれいです。

畳の部屋があります。

布団で寝ます。

初めての経験です。

よく眠れました。

Comprehension Question

- ジョンさんは何で寝ますか？
  (What does John sleep on?)

Story with Line-by-Line Breakdown

ジョンさんは友達の家に泊まります。

- **Japanese:** ジョンさんは友達の家に泊まります。

- **Romaji:** Jon-san wa tomodachi no ie ni tomarimasu.

- **English:** John stays at his friend's house.

Grammar and Vocabulary:

- 友達の家 (tomodachi no ie): friend's house; "の" indicates possession.

- に (ni): indicates location.

- 泊まります (tomarimasu): to stay overnight; polite form.

日本の家はとてもきれいです。

- **Japanese:** 日本の家はとてもきれいです。

- **Romaji:** Nihon no ie wa totemo kirei desu.

- **English:** The Japanese house is very clean.

Grammar and Vocabulary:

- 日本の家 **(Nihon no ie):** Japanese house; "の" indicates possession.

- とても **(totemo):** very.

- きれい **(kirei):** clean/beautiful; "na" adjective.

- です **(desu):** polite sentence ending.

畳の部屋があります。

- **Japanese:** 畳の部屋があります。

- **Romaji:** Tatami no heya ga arimasu.

- **English:** There is a tatami room.

Grammar and Vocabulary:

- 畳 **(tatami):** traditional Japanese mat.

- 部屋 **(heya):** room.

- が **(ga):** subject marker.

- あります **(arimasu):** to exist; used for non-living things.

布団で寝ます。

- **Japanese:** 布団で寝ます。

- **Romaji:** Futon de nemasu.

- **English:** He sleeps on a futon.

Grammar and Vocabulary:

- 布団 **(futon):** Japanese bedding.

- で **(de):** indicates the means.

- 寝ます **(nemasu):** to sleep; polite form.

初めての経験です。

- **Japanese:** 初めての経験です。

- **Romaji:** Hajimete no keiken desu.

- **English:** It's a first-time experience.

Grammar and Vocabulary:

- 初めて **(hajimete):** first time.

- 経験 **(keiken):** experience.

- です **(desu):** polite sentence ending.

よく眠れました。

- **Japanese:** よく眠れました。

- **Romaji:** Yoku nemuremashita.

- **English:** He slept well.

Grammar and Vocabulary:

- よく **(yoku):** well.

- 眠れました **(nemuremashita):** could sleep (past polite form of "nemureru" - to be able to sleep).

Story 24: 茶道を体験する
(Experiencing the Tea Ceremony)

Story in Japanese

ジョンさんは茶道を体験します。

先生がお茶の入れ方を教えてくれます。

お茶は少し苦いです。

でも、とても美味しいです。

礼儀を学びます。

貴重な経験でした。

Comprehension Question

- ジョンさんは何を学びますか？
  (What does John learn?)

Story with Line-by-Line Breakdown

ジョンさんは茶道を体験します。

- **Japanese:** ジョンさんは茶道を体験します。

- **Romaji:** Jon-san wa sadou o taiken shimasu.

- **English:** John experiences the tea ceremony.

Grammar and Vocabulary:

- 茶道 **(sadou):** tea ceremony.

- を **(o):** object marker.

- 体験します **(taiken shimasu):** to experience; polite form.

先生がお茶の入れ方を教えてくれます。

- **Japanese:** 先生がお茶の入れ方を教えてくれます。

- **Romaji:** Sensei ga ocha no irekata o oshiete kuremasu.

- **English:** The teacher shows him how to make tea.

Grammar and Vocabulary:

- 先生 **(sensei):** teacher.

- お茶の入れ方 **(ocha no irekata):** way of making tea.

- を **(o):** object marker.

- 教えてくれます **(oshiete kuremasu):** to teach/show (favor for the listener).

お茶は少し苦いです。

- **Japanese:** お茶は少し苦いです。

- **Romaji:** Ocha wa sukoshi nigai desu.

- **English:** The tea is a little bitter.

Grammar and Vocabulary:

- お茶 **(ocha):** tea.

- 少し **(sukoshi):** a little.

- 苦い **(nigai):** bitter; "i" adjective.

- です **(desu):** polite sentence ending.

でも、とても美味しいです。

- **Japanese:** でも、とても美味しいです。

- **Romaji:** Demo, totemo oishii desu.

- **English:** But it's very delicious.

Grammar and Vocabulary:

- でも **(demo):** but.

- とても **(totemo):** very.

- 美味しい **(oishii):** delicious; "i" adjective.

- です **(desu):** polite sentence ending.

礼儀を学びます。

- **Japanese:** 礼儀を学びます。

- **Romaji:** Reigi o manabimasu.

- **English:** He learns etiquette.

Grammar and Vocabulary:

- 礼儀 **(reigi):** etiquette/manners.

- を **(o):** object marker.

- 学びます **(manabimasu):** to learn; polite form.

貴重な経験でした。

- **Japanese:** 貴重な経験でした。

- **Romaji:** Kichou na keiken deshita.

- **English:** It was a valuable experience.

Grammar and Vocabulary:

- 貴重な **(kichou na):** valuable/precious; "na" adjective.

- 経験 **(keiken):** experience.

- でした **(deshita):** past polite form of "です" (desu).

Story 25: 書道を習う (Learning Calligraphy)

Story in Japanese

ジョンさんは書道を習います。

筆と墨を使います。

漢字を書きます。

「友」という字を書きます。

難しいですが、面白いです。

出来上がった作品を持ち帰ります。

Comprehension Question

- ジョンさんはどんな字を書きますか？
  (What character does John write?)

Story with Line-by-Line Breakdown

ジョンさんは書道を習います。

- **Japanese:** ジョンさんは書道を習います。

- **Romaji:** Jon-san wa shodou o naraimasu.

- **English:** John learns calligraphy.

Grammar and Vocabulary:

- 書道 **(shodou):** calligraphy.

- を **(o):** object marker.

- 習います **(naraimasu):** to learn; polite form.

筆と墨を使います。

- **Japanese:** 筆と墨を使います。

- **Romaji:** Fude to sumi o tsukaimasu.

- **English:** He uses a brush and ink.

Grammar and Vocabulary:

- 筆 **(fude):** brush.

- 墨 **(sumi):** ink.

- と **(to):** and.

- を **(o):** object marker.

- 使います **(tsukaimasu):** to use; polite form.

漢字を書きます。

- **Japanese:** 漢字を書きます。

- **Romaji:** Kanji o kakimasu.

- **English:** He writes kanji.

Grammar and Vocabulary:

- 漢字 **(kanji):** kanji (Chinese character used in Japanese).

- を **(o):** object marker.

- 書きます **(kakimasu):** to write; polite form.

「友」という字を書きます。

- **Japanese:** 「友」という字を書きます。

- **Romaji:** "Tomodachi" to iu ji o kakimasu.

- **English:** He writes the character for "friend."

Grammar and Vocabulary:

- 友 **(tomo):** friend.

- という **(to iu):** called/named.

- 字 **(ji):** character.

- を **(o):** object marker.

- 書きます **(kakimasu):** to write; polite form.

難しいですが、面白いです。

- **Japanese:** 難しいですが、面白いです。

- **Romaji:** Muzukashii desu ga, omoshiroi desu.

- **English:** It's difficult, but interesting.

Grammar and Vocabulary:

- 難しい **(muzukashii):** difficult; "i" adjective.

- ですが **(desu ga):** but (polite form).

- 面白い **(omoshiroi):** interesting; "i" adjective.

出来上がった作品を持ち帰ります。

- **Japanese:** 出来上がった作品を持ち帰ります。

- **Romaji:** Dekiagatta sakuhin o mochikaerimasu.

- **English:** He takes home his completed work.

Grammar and Vocabulary:

- 出来上がった **(dekiagatta):** completed/finished.

- 作品 **(sakuhin):** work/piece.

- を **(o):** object marker.

- 持ち帰ります **(mochikaerimasu):** to take home; polite form.

Story 26: 富士山を見る (Seeing Mount Fuji)

Story in Japanese

ジョンさんは富士山を見に行きます。

富士山はとても高い山です。

頂上には雪があります。

美しい景色です。

ジョンさんは感動します。

友達に写真を送ります。

Comprehension Question

- ジョンさんは富士山のどこに雪があるのを見ますか？
  (Where does John see snow on Mount Fuji?)

Story with Line-by-Line Breakdown

ジョンさんは富士山を見に行きます。

- **Japanese:** ジョンさんは富士山を見に行きます。

- **Romaji:** Jon-san wa Fujisan o mi ni ikimasu.

- **English:** John goes to see Mount Fuji.

Grammar and Vocabulary:

- 富士山 **(Fujisan):** Mount Fuji.

- を **(o):** object marker.

- 見に行きます **(mi ni ikimasu):** to go to see; polite form.

富士山はとても高い山です。

- **Japanese:** 富士山はとても高い山です。

- **Romaji:** Fujisan wa totemo takai yama desu.

- **English:** Mount Fuji is a very tall mountain.

- とても **(totemo):** very.

- 高い **(takai):** tall/high; "i" adjective.

- 山 **(yama):** mountain.

- です **(desu):** polite sentence ending.

頂上には雪があります。

- **Japanese:** 頂上には雪があります。

- **Romaji:** Choujou ni wa yuki ga arimasu.

- **English:** There is snow at the summit.

Grammar and Vocabulary:

- 頂上 **(choujou):** summit/top.

- には **(ni wa):** combination of "ni" (indicating location) and "wa" (topic marker).

- 雪 **(yuki):** snow.

- が **(ga):** subject marker.

- あります **(arimasu):** to exist; used for non-living things.

美しい景色です。

- **Japanese:** 美しい景色です。

- **Romaji:** Utsukushii keshiki desu.

- **English:** It's a beautiful view.

Grammar and Vocabulary:

- 美しい **(utsukushii):** beautiful; "i" adjective.

- 景色 **(keshiki):** scenery/view.

- です **(desu):** polite sentence ending.

ジョンさんは感動します。

- **Japanese:** ジョンさんは感動します。

- **Romaji:** Jon-san wa kandou shimasu.

- **English:** John is moved.

Grammar and Vocabulary:

- 感動します **(kandou shimasu):** to be moved/touched; polite form.

友達に写真を送ります。

- **Japanese:** 友達に写真を送ります。

- **Romaji:** Tomodachi ni shashin o okurimasu.

- **English:** He sends a photo to his friend.

Grammar and Vocabulary:

- 友達に **(tomodachi ni):** to his friend; "に" indicates the recipient.

- 写真 **(shashin):** photo.

- を **(o):** object marker.

- 送ります **(okurimasu):** to send; polite form.

Story 27: 日本の学校を訪問 (Visiting a Japanese School)

Story in Japanese

ジョンさんは日本の学校を訪問します。

生徒たちは元気です。

授業を見学します。

みんな一生けん命勉強しています。

校庭で一緒に遊びます。

楽しい時間を過ごしました。

Comprehension Question

- ジョンさんはどこで生徒たちと遊びますか？
  (Where does John play with the students?)

Story with Line-by-Line Breakdown

ジョンさんは日本の学校を訪問します。

- **Japanese:** ジョンさんは日本の学校を訪問します。

- **Romaji:** Jon-san wa Nihon no gakkou o houmon shimasu.

- **English:** John visits a Japanese school.

Grammar and Vocabulary:

- 日本の学校 **(Nihon no gakkou):** Japanese school; "の" indicates possession.

- を **(o):** object marker.

- 訪問します **(houmon shimasu):** to visit; polite form.

生徒たちは元気です。

- **Japanese:** 生徒たちは元気です。

- **Romaji:** Seito-tachi wa genki desu.

- **English:** The students are energetic.

Grammar and Vocabulary:

- 生徒たち **(seito-tachi):** students; "たち" pluralizes "生徒" (student).

- 元気 **(genki):** energetic/healthy.

- です **(desu):** polite sentence ending.

授業を見学します。

- **Japanese:** 授業を見学します。

- **Romaji:** Jugyou o kengaku shimasu.

- **English:** He observes a class.

Grammar and Vocabulary:

- 授業 **(jugyou):** class/lesson.

- を **(o):** object marker.

- 見学します **(kengaku shimasu):** to observe; polite form.

みんな一生けん命勉強しています。

- **Japanese:** みんな一生けん命勉強しています。

- **Romaji:** Minna isshoukenmei benkyou shiteimasu.

- **English:** Everyone is studying hard.

Grammar and Vocabulary:

- みんな **(minna):** everyone.

- 一生けん命 **(isshoukenmei):** diligently/with all effort.

- 勉強しています **(benkyou shiteimasu):** is studying; polite continuous form.

校庭で一緒に遊びます。

- **Japanese:** 校庭で一緒に遊びます。

- **Romaji:** Koutei de issho ni asobimasu.

- **English:** They play together in the schoolyard.

Grammar and Vocabulary:

- 校庭 **(koutei):** schoolyard.

- で **(de):** indicates location.

- 一緒に **(issho ni):** together.

- 遊びます **(asobimasu):** to play; polite form.

楽しい時間を過ごしました。

- **Japanese:** 楽しい時間を過ごしました。

- **Romaji:** Tanoshii jikan o sugoshimashita.

- **English:** He spent an enjoyable time.

Grammar and Vocabulary:

- 楽しい **(tanoshii):** enjoyable/fun; "i" adjective.

- 時間 **(jikan):** time.

- を **(o):** object marker.

- 過ごしました **(sugoshimashita):** spent (past polite form of "sugosu" - to spend time).

Story 28: 電子製品を買う (Buying Electronics)

Story in Japanese

ジョンさんは秋葉原に行きます。

たくさんの電子製品があります。

新しいカメラを買います。

店員さんが説明してくれます。

日本の技術はすごいです。

買い物に満足です。

Comprehension Question

- ジョンさんは何を買いますか？
  (What does John buy?)

Story with Line-by-Line Breakdown

ジョンさんは秋葉原に行きます。

- **Japanese:** ジョンさんは秋葉原に行きます。

- **Romaji:** Jon-san wa Akihabara ni ikimasu.

- **English:** John goes to Akihabara.

Grammar and Vocabulary:

- 秋葉原 **(Akihabara):** Akihabara, a district in Tokyo known for electronics.

- に **(ni):** indicates the destination.

- 行きます **(ikimasu):** to go; polite form.

たくさんの電子製品があります。

- **Japanese:** たくさんの電子製品があります。

- **Romaji:** Takusan no denshi seihin ga arimasu.

- **English:** There are many electronic products.

Grammar and Vocabulary:

- たくさんの **(takusan no):** many/lots of.

- 電子製品 **(denshi seihin):** electronic products.

- が **(ga):** subject marker.

- あります **(arimasu):** to exist; used for non-living things.

新しいカメラを買います。

- **Japanese:** 新しいカメラを買います。

- **Romaji:** Atarashii kamera o kaimasu.

- **English:** He buys a new camera.

Grammar and Vocabulary:

- 新しい **(atarashii):** new; "i" adjective.

- カメラ **(kamera):** camera.

- を **(o):** object marker.

- 買います **(kaimasu):** to buy; polite form.

店員さんが説明してくれます。

- **Japanese:** 店員さんが説明してくれます。

- **Romaji:** Ten'in-san ga setsumei shite kuremasu.

- **English:** The store clerk explains to him.

Grammar and Vocabulary:

- 店員さん **(ten'in-san):** store clerk; "さん" is an honorific.

- が **(ga):** subject marker.

- 説明してくれます **(setsumei shite kuremasu):** explains (as a favor to the listener).

日本の技術はすごいです。

- **Japanese:** 日本の技術はすごいです。

- **Romaji:** Nihon no gijutsu wa sugoi desu.

- **English:** Japanese technology is amazing.

Grammar and Vocabulary:

- 日本の技術 **(Nihon no gijutsu):** Japanese technology; "の" indicates possession.

- は **(wa):** topic marker.

- すごい **(sugoi):** amazing; "i" adjective.

- です **(desu):** polite sentence ending.

買い物に満足です。

- **Japanese:** 買い物に満足です。

- **Romaji:** Kaimono ni manzoku desu.

- **English:** He is satisfied with his shopping.

Grammar and Vocabulary:

- 買い物 **(kaimono):** shopping.

- に **(ni):** indicates the target of satisfaction.

- 満足 **(manzoku):** satisfaction/contentment.

- です **(desu):** polite sentence ending.

Story 29: カラオケに行く (Going to Karaoke)

Story in Japanese

夜、ジョンさんはカラオケに行きます。

友達と一緒です。

日本の歌を歌います。

みんなで盛り上がります。

楽しい夜でした。

また行きたいです。

Comprehension Question

- ジョンさんは誰とカラオケに行きますか？
  (Who does John go to karaoke with?)

Story with Line-by-Line Breakdown

夜、ジョンさんはカラオケに行きます。

- **Japanese:** 夜、ジョンさんはカラオケに行きます。

- **Romaji:** Yoru, Jon-san wa karaoke ni ikimasu.

- **English:** In the evening, John goes to karaoke.

Grammar and Vocabulary:

- 夜 **(yoru):** evening/night.

- カラオケ **(karaoke):** karaoke.

- に **(ni):** indicates the destination.

- 行きます **(ikimasu):** to go; polite form.

友達と一緒です。

- **Japanese:** 友達と一緒です。

- **Romaji:** Tomodachi to issho desu.

- **English:** He is with friends.

Grammar and Vocabulary:

- 友達 **(tomodachi):** friend(s).

- と **(to):** with.

- 一緒 **(issho):** together.

- です **(desu):** polite sentence ending.

日本の歌を歌います。

- **Japanese:** 日本の歌を歌います。

- **Romaji:** Nihon no uta o utaimasu.

- **English:** He sings Japanese songs.

Grammar and Vocabulary:

- 日本の歌 **(Nihon no uta):** Japanese song(s); "の" indicates possession.

- を **(o):** object marker.

- 歌います **(utaimasu):** to sing; polite form.

みんなで盛り上がります。

- **Japanese:** みんなで盛り上がります。

- **Romaji:** Minna de moriagarimasu.

- **English:** Everyone gets excited.

Grammar and Vocabulary:

- みんなで **(minna de):** with everyone.

- 盛り上がります **(moriagarimasu):** to get excited; polite form.

楽しい夜でした。

- **Japanese:** 楽しい夜でした。

- **Romaji:** Tanoshii yoru deshita.

- **English:** It was a fun night.

Grammar and Vocabulary:

- 楽しい **(tanoshii):** fun/enjoyable; "i" adjective.

- 夜 **(yoru):** night.

- でした **(deshita):** past polite form of "です" (desu).

また行きたいです。

- **Japanese:** また行きたいです。

- **Romaji:** Mata ikitai desu.

- **English:** He wants to go again.

Grammar and Vocabulary:

- また **(mata):** again.

- 行きたい **(ikitai):** want to go (using "たい" form for expressing desire).

- です **(desu):** polite sentence ending.

Story 30: お寺で瞑想 (Meditating at a Temple)

Story in Japanese

ジョンさんはお寺に行きます。

静かな場所です。

瞑想をします。

心が落ち着きます。

お坊さんと話をします。

良い時間を過ごしました。

Comprehension Question

- ジョンさんはお寺で何をしますか？
  (What does John do at the temple?)

Story with Line-by-Line Breakdown

ジョンさんはお寺に行きます。

- **Japanese:** ジョンさんはお寺に行きます。

- **Romaji:** Jon-san wa otera ni ikimasu.

- **English:** John goes to the temple.

Grammar and Vocabulary:

- お寺 **(otera):** temple; "お" is an honorific prefix for politeness.

- に **(ni):** indicates the destination.

- 行きます **(ikimasu):** to go; polite form.

静かな場所です。

- **Japanese:** 静かな場所です。

- **Romaji:** Shizuka na basho desu.

- **English:** It's a quiet place.

Grammar and Vocabulary:

- 静かな **(shizuka na):** quiet; "na" adjective.

- 場所 **(basho):** place.

- です **(desu):** polite sentence ending.

瞑想をします。

- **Japanese:** 瞑想をします。

- **Romaji:** Meisou o shimasu.

- **English:** He meditates.

Grammar and Vocabulary:

- 瞑想 **(meisou):** meditation.

- を **(o):** object marker.

- します **(shimasu):** to do; polite form.

心が落ち着きます。

- **Japanese:** 心が落ち着きます。

- **Romaji:** Kokoro ga ochitsukimasu.

- **English:** His mind feels calm.

Grammar and Vocabulary:

- 心 **(kokoro):** mind/heart.

- が **(ga):** subject marker.

- 落ち着きます **(ochitsukimasu):** to feel calm; polite form.

お坊さんと話をします。

- **Japanese:** お坊さんと話をします。

- **Romaji:** Obousan to hanashi o shimasu.
- **English:** He talks with a monk.

Grammar and Vocabulary:

- お坊さん **(obousan):** monk; "お" is an honorific prefix.
- と **(to):** with.
- 話をします **(hanashi o shimasu):** to talk; polite form.

良い時間を過ごしました。

- **Japanese:** 良い時間を過ごしました。
- **Romaji:** Yoi jikan o sugoshimashita.
- **English:** He spent a good time.

Grammar and Vocabulary:

- 良い **(yoi):** good; "i" adjective.
- 時間 **(jikan):** time.
- を **(o):** object marker.
- 過ごしました **(sugoshimashita):** spent (past polite form of "sugosu" - to spend time).

Story 31: 新幹線に乗る (Riding the Shinkansen)

Story in Japanese

ジョンさんは新幹線に乗ります。

速い電車です。

窓<ruby>まど</ruby>から景色<ruby>けしき</ruby>を見<ruby>み</ruby>ます。

座席<ruby>ざせき</ruby>は快適<ruby>かいてき</ruby>です。

京都<ruby>きょうと</ruby>に行<ruby>い</ruby>きます。

旅行<ruby>りょこう</ruby>が楽<ruby>たの</ruby>しみです。

Comprehension Question

- ジョンさんは新幹線でどこに行きますか？
  (Where does John go on the Shinkansen?)

Story with Line-by-Line Breakdown

ジョンさんは新幹線に乗ります。

- **Japanese:** ジョンさんは新幹線に乗ります。

- **Romaji:** Jon-san wa shinkansen ni norimasu.

- **English:** John rides the Shinkansen.

Grammar and Vocabulary:

- 新幹線 **(shinkansen):** Shinkansen (Japanese bullet train).

- に **(ni):** indicates the vehicle being boarded.

- 乗ります **(norimasu):** to ride; polite form.

速い電車です。

- **Japanese:** 速い電車です。

- **Romaji:** Hayai densha desu.

- **English:** It's a fast train.

Grammar and Vocabulary:

- 速い **(hayai):** fast; "i" adjective.

- 電車 **(densha):** train.

- です **(desu):** polite sentence ending.

窓から景色を見ます。

- **Japanese:** 窓から景色を見ます。

- **Romaji:** Mado kara keshiki o mimasu.

- **English:** He looks at the scenery from the window.

Grammar and Vocabulary:

- 窓 **(mado):** window.

- から **(kara):** from.

- 景色 **(keshiki):** scenery/view.

- を **(o):** object marker.

- 見ます **(mimasu):** to look at; polite form.

座席は快適です。

- **Japanese:** 座席は快適です。

- **Romaji:** Zaseki wa kaiteki desu.

- **English:** The seat is comfortable.

Grammar and Vocabulary:

- 座席 **(zaseki):** seat.

- は **(wa):** topic marker.

- 快適 **(kaiteki):** comfortable.

- です **(desu):** polite sentence ending.

京都に行きます。

- **Japanese:** 京都に行きます。

- **Romaji:** Kyouto ni ikimasu.

- **English:** He goes to Kyoto.

Grammar and Vocabulary:

- 京都 **(Kyouto):** Kyoto.

- に **(ni):** indicates the destination.

- 行きます **(ikimasu):** to go; polite form.

旅行が楽しみです。

- **Japanese:** 旅行が楽しみです。

- **Romaji:** Ryokou ga tanoshimi desu.

- **English:** He is looking forward to the trip.

Grammar and Vocabulary:

- 旅行 **(ryokou):** trip/travel.

- が **(ga):** subject marker.

- 楽しみ **(tanoshimi):** looking forward/anticipation.

- です **(desu):** polite sentence ending.

Story 32: 京都を散策 (Exploring Kyoto)

Story in Japanese

ジョンさんは京都を歩きます。

古い町並みがあります。

お寺や神社がたくさんあります。

日本の伝統を感じます。

お土産を買います。

素敵な一日でした。

Comprehension Question

- ジョンさんは京都で何を感じますか？
  (What does John feel in Kyoto?)

Story with Line-by-Line Breakdown

ジョンさんは京都を歩きます。

- **Japanese:** ジョンさんは京都を歩きます。

- **Romaji:** Jon-san wa Kyouto o arukimasu.

- **English:** John walks around Kyoto.

Grammar and Vocabulary:

- 京都 **(Kyouto):** Kyoto.

- を **(o):** object marker.

- 歩きます **(arukimasu):** to walk; polite form.

古い町並みがあります。

- **Japanese:** 古い町並みがあります。

- **Romaji:** Furui machinami ga arimasu.

- **English:** There are old townscapes.

Grammar and Vocabulary:

- 古い **(furui):** old; "i" adjective.

- 町並み **(machinami):** townscape/streetscape.

- が **(ga):** subject marker.

- あります **(arimasu):** to exist; used for non-living things.

お寺や神社がたくさんあります。

- **Japanese:** お寺や神社がたくさんあります。

- **Romaji:** Otera ya jinja ga takusan arimasu.

- **English:** There are many temples and shrines.

Grammar and Vocabulary:

- お寺 **(otera):** temple.

- 神社 **(jinja):** shrine.

- や **(ya):** and (used for listing examples).

- たくさん **(takusan):** many.

- あります **(arimasu):** to exist; used for non-living things.

日本の伝統を感じます。

- **Japanese:** 日本の伝統を感じます。

- **Romaji:** Nihon no dentou o kanjimasu.

- **English:** He feels the Japanese tradition.

Grammar and Vocabulary:

- 日本の伝統 **(Nihon no dentou):** Japanese tradition; "の" indicates possession.

- を **(o):** object marker.

- 感じます **(kanjimasu):** to feel; polite form.

お土産を買います。

- **Japanese:** お土産を買います。

- **Romaji:** Omiyage o kaimasu.

- **English:** He buys souvenirs.

Grammar and Vocabulary:

- お土産 **(omiyage):** souvenir.

- を **(o):** object marker.

- 買います **(kaimasu):** to buy; polite form.

素敵な一日でした。

- **Japanese:** 素敵な一日でした。

- **Romaji:** Suteki na ichinichi deshita.

- **English:** It was a wonderful day.

Grammar and Vocabulary:

- 素敵な **(suteki na):** wonderful/lovely; "na" adjective.

- 一日 **(ichinichi):** one day.

- でした **(deshita):** past polite form of "です" (desu).

Story 33: 和菓子を作る (Making Japanese Sweets)

Story in Japanese

ジョンさんは和菓子作りを体験します。

先生が教えてくれます。

お餅を作ります。

形を作って、色をつけます。

出来上がった和菓子を食べます。

とても美味しいです。

Comprehension Question

- ジョンさんは何を作りますか？
  (What does John make?)

Story with Line-by-Line Breakdown

ジョンさんは和菓子作りを体験します。

- **Japanese:** ジョンさんは和菓子作りを体験します。

- **Romaji:** Jon-san wa wagashi-zukuri o taiken shimasu.

- **English:** John experiences making Japanese sweets.

Grammar and Vocabulary:

- 和菓子作り **(wagashi-zukuri):** making Japanese sweets; "和菓子" means Japanese sweets, "作り" means making.

- を **(o):** object marker.

- 体験します **(taiken shimasu):** to experience; polite form.

先生が教えてくれます。

- **Japanese:** 先生が教えてくれます。

- **Romaji:** Sensei ga oshiete kuremasu.

- **English:** The teacher teaches him.

Grammar and Vocabulary:

- 先生 **(sensei):** teacher.

- が **(ga):** subject marker.

- 教えてくれます **(oshiete kuremasu):** to teach/explain as a favor to the listener.

お餅を作ります。

- **Japanese:** お餅を作ります。

- **Romaji:** Omochi o tsukurimasu.

- **English:** He makes mochi.

Grammar and Vocabulary:

- お餅 **(omochi):** mochi (rice cake).

- を **(o):** object marker.

- 作ります **(tsukurimasu):** to make; polite form.

形を作って、色をつけます。

- **Japanese:** 形を作って、色をつけます。

- **Romaji:** Katachi o tsukutte, iro o tsukemasu.

- **English:** He shapes it and adds color.

Grammar and Vocabulary:

- 形 **(katachi):** shape/form.

- を作って **(o tsukutte):** to make (shape); "て" form connects sequential actions.

- 色 **(iro):** color.

- をつけます **(o tsukemasu):** to add color; polite form.

出来上がった和菓子を食べます。

- **Japanese:** 出来上がった和菓子を食べます。

- **Romaji:** Dekiagatta wagashi o tabemasu.

- **English:** He eats the finished Japanese sweets.

Grammar and Vocabulary:

- 出来上がった **(dekiagatta):** completed/finished.

- 和菓子 **(wagashi):** Japanese sweets.

- を **(o):** object marker.

- 食べます **(tabemasu):** to eat; polite form.

とても美味しいです。

- **Japanese:** とても美味しいです。

- **Romaji:** Totemo oishii desu.

- **English:** It's very delicious.

Grammar and Vocabulary:

- とても **(totemo):** very.

- 美味しい **(oishii):** delicious; "i" adjective.

- です **(desu):** polite sentence ending.

Story 34: 友達と再会 (Reuniting with a Friend)

Story in Japanese

ジョンさんは昔の友達と会います。

一緒に昼ごはんを食べます。

話 がはずみます。

公園を散歩します。

楽しい時間を過ごしました。

また会いましょうと言います。

Comprehension Question

- ジョンさんは友達と何を食べますか？
  (What does John eat with his friend?)

Story with Line-by-Line Breakdown

ジョンさんは昔の友達と会います。

- **Japanese:** ジョンさんは昔の友達と会います。

- **Romaji:** Jon-san wa mukashi no tomodachi to aimasu.

- **English:** John meets an old friend.

Grammar and Vocabulary:

- 昔の友達 **(mukashi no tomodachi):** old friend; "の" indicates possession.

- と **(to):** with.

- 会います **(aimasu):** to meet; polite form.

一緒に昼ごはんを食べます。

- **Japanese:** 一緒に昼ごはんを食べます。

- **Romaji:** Issho ni hirugohan o tabemasu.

- **English:** They eat lunch together.

Grammar and Vocabulary:

- 一緒に **(issho ni):** together.

- 昼ごはん **(hirugohan):** lunch.

- を **(o):** object marker.

- 食べます **(tabemasu):** to eat; polite form.

話がはずみます。

- **Japanese:** 話がはずみます。

- **Romaji:** Hanashi ga hazumimasu.

- **English:** The conversation flows.

Grammar and Vocabulary:

- 話 **(hanashi):** conversation/talk.

- が **(ga):** subject marker.

- はずみます **(hazumimasu):** to liven up; polite form.

公園を散歩します。

- **Japanese:** 公園を散歩します。

- **Romaji:** Kouen o sanpo shimasu.

- **English:** They take a walk in the park.

Grammar and Vocabulary:

- 公園 **(kouen):** park.

- を **(o):** object marker.

- 散歩します **(sanpo shimasu):** to take a walk; polite form.

楽しい時間を過ごしました。

- **Japanese:** 楽しい時間を過ごしました。

- **Romaji:** Tanoshii jikan o sugoshimashita.

- **English:** They spent an enjoyable time.

Grammar and Vocabulary:

- 楽しい **(tanoshii):** enjoyable/fun; "i" adjective.

- 時間 **(jikan):** time.

- を **(o):** object marker.

- 過ごしました **(sugoshimashita):** spent (past polite form of "sugosu" - to spend time).

また会いましょうと言います。

- **Japanese:** また会いましょうと言います。

- **Romaji:** Mata aimashou to iimasu.

- **English:** They say, "Let's meet again."

Grammar and Vocabulary:

- また **(mata):** again.

- 会いましょう **(aimashou):** let's meet; "ましょう" indicates a suggestion or invitation.

- と言います **(to iimasu):** to say (indirect quote marker "と" + "言います" to say).

Story 35: 日本の祭りに参加
(Participating in a Japanese Festival)

Story in Japanese

ジョンさんは祭りに参加します。

みこしを見ます。

踊りを見ます。

屋台で食べ物を買います。

とてもにぎやかです。

思い出に残る経験です。

Comprehension Question

- ジョンさんは祭りで何を見ますか？
  (What does John see at the festival?)

Story with Line-by-Line Breakdown

ジョンさんは祭りに参加します。

- **Japanese:** ジョンさんは祭りに参加します。

- **Romaji:** Jon-san wa matsuri ni sanka shimasu.

- **English:** John participates in the festival.

Grammar and Vocabulary:

- 祭り **(matsuri):** festival.

- に **(ni):** indicates participation or involvement.

- 参加します **(sanka shimasu):** to participate; polite form.

みこしを見ます。

- **Japanese:** みこしを見ます。

- **Romaji:** Mikoshi o mimasu.

- **English:** He sees a portable shrine.

Grammar and Vocabulary:

- みこし **(mikoshi):** portable shrine (carried during festivals).

- を **(o):** object marker.

- 見ます **(mimasu):** to see; polite form.

踊りを見ます。

- **Japanese:** 踊りを見ます。

- **Romaji:** Odori o mimasu.

- **English:** He watches the dances.

Grammar and Vocabulary:

- 踊り **(odori):** dance.

- を **(o):** object marker.

- 見ます **(mimasu):** to watch/see; polite form.

屋台で食べ物を買います。

- **Japanese:** 屋台で食べ物を買います。

- **Romaji:** Yatai de tabemono o kaimasu.

- **English:** He buys food at a food stall.

Grammar and Vocabulary:

- 屋台 **(yatai):** food stall.

- で **(de):** indicates the place of action.

- 食べ物 **(tabemono):** food.

- を **(o):** object marker.

- 買います **(kaimasu):** to buy; polite form.

とてもにぎやかです。

- **Japanese:** とてもにぎやかです。

- **Romaji:** Totemo nigiyaka desu.

- **English:** It's very lively.

Grammar and Vocabulary:

- とても **(totemo):** very.

- にぎやか **(nigiyaka):** lively; "na" adjective.

- です **(desu):** polite sentence ending.

思い出に残る経験です。

- **Japanese:** 思い出に残る経験です。

- **Romaji:** Omoide ni nokoru keiken desu.

- **English:** It's a memorable experience.

Grammar and Vocabulary:

- 思い出に残る **(omoide ni nokoru):** memorable (lit. "remains in memory").

- 経験 **(keiken):** experience.

- です **(desu):** polite sentence ending.

Story 36: 浴衣を着る (Wearing a Yukata)

Story in Japanese

ジョンさんは浴衣を着ます。

友達が手伝ってくれます。

夏祭りに行きます。

浴衣は涼しくて快適です。

写真をたくさん撮ります。

日本の夏を楽しみます。

Comprehension Question

- ジョンさんはどこに浴衣を着て行きますか？
  (Where does John go wearing a yukata?)

Story with Line-by-Line Breakdown

ジョンさんは浴衣を着ます。

- **Japanese:** ジョンさんは浴衣を着ます。

- **Romaji:** Jon-san wa yukata o kimasu.

- **English:** John wears a yukata.

Grammar and Vocabulary:

- 浴衣 **(yukata):** yukata (a casual summer kimono).

- を **(o):** object marker.

- 着ます **(kimasu):** to wear; polite form.

友達が手伝ってくれます。

- **Japanese:** 友達が手伝ってくれます。

- **Romaji:** Tomodachi ga tetsudatte kuremasu.

- **English:** His friend helps him.

Grammar and Vocabulary:

- 友達 **(tomodachi):** friend.

- が **(ga):** subject marker.

- 手伝ってくれます **(tetsudatte kuremasu):** to help as a favor; polite form.

夏祭りに行きます。

- **Japanese:** 夏祭りに行きます。

- **Romaji:** Natsumatsuri ni ikimasu.

- **English:** He goes to the summer festival.

Grammar and Vocabulary:

- 夏祭り **(natsumatsuri):** summer festival.

- に **(ni):** indicates destination.

- 行きます **(ikimasu):** to go; polite form.

浴衣は涼しくて快適です。

- **Japanese:** 浴衣は涼しくて快適です。

- **Romaji:** Yukata wa suzushikute kaiteki desu.

- **English:** The yukata is cool and comfortable.

Grammar and Vocabulary:

- 涼しくて **(suzushikute):** cool; "て" form connects adjectives.

- 快適 **(kaiteki):** comfortable; "na" adjective.

- です **(desu):** polite sentence ending.

写真をたくさん撮ります。

- **Japanese:** 写真をたくさん撮ります。

- **Romaji:** Shashin o takusan torimasu.

- **English:** He takes many photos.

Grammar and Vocabulary:

- 写真 **(shashin):** photo.

- を **(o):** object marker.

- たくさん **(takusan):** many/a lot.

- 撮ります **(torimasu):** to take (a photo); polite form.

日本の夏を楽しみます。

- **Japanese:** 日本の夏を楽しみます。

- **Romaji:** Nihon no natsu o tanoshimimasu.

- **English:** He enjoys the Japanese summer.

Grammar and Vocabulary:

- 日本の夏 **(Nihon no natsu):** Japanese summer; "の" indicates possession.

- を **(o):** object marker.

- 楽しみます **(tanoshimimasu):** to enjoy; polite form.

Story 37: 花火大会を見る (Watching the Fireworks Festival)

Story in Japanese

ジョンさんは花火大会に行きます。

夜空に大きな花火が上がります。

とてもきれいです。

人<ruby>人<rt>ひと</rt></ruby>がたくさんいます。

友達<ruby>友達<rt>ともだち</rt></ruby>と<ruby>一緒<rt>いっしょ</rt></ruby>に<ruby>見<rt>み</rt></ruby>ます。

<ruby>素晴<rt>すば</rt></ruby>らしい<ruby>夜<rt>よる</rt></ruby>でした。

Comprehension Question

- ジョンさんは誰と花火を見ますか？
  (Who does John watch the fireworks with?)

Story with Line-by-Line Breakdown

ジョンさんは花火大会に行きます。

- **Japanese:** ジョンさんは花火大会に行きます。

- **Romaji:** Jon-san wa hanabi taikai ni ikimasu.

- **English:** John goes to the fireworks festival.

Grammar and Vocabulary:

- 花火大会 **(hanabi taikai):** fireworks festival.

- に **(ni):** indicates the destination.

- 行きます **(ikimasu):** to go; polite form.

夜空に大きな花火が上がります。

- **Japanese:** 夜空に大きな花火が上がります。

- **Romaji:** Yozora ni ookina hanabi ga agarimasu.

- **English:** Large fireworks rise in the night sky.

Grammar and Vocabulary:

- 夜空 **(yozora):** night sky.

- に **(ni):** indicates location.

- 大きな **(ookina):** large/big.

- 花火 **(hanabi):** fireworks.

- が **(ga):** subject marker.

- 上がります **(agarimasu):** to rise; polite form.

とてもきれいです。

- **Japanese:** とてもきれいです。

- **Romaji:** Totemo kirei desu.

- **English:** It's very beautiful.

Grammar and Vocabulary:

- とても **(totemo):** very.

- きれい **(kirei):** beautiful; "na" adjective.

- です **(desu):** polite sentence ending.

人がたくさんいます。

- **Japanese:** 人がたくさんいます。

- **Romaji:** Hito ga takusan imasu.

- **English:** There are many people.

Grammar and Vocabulary:

- 人 **(hito):** people.

- が **(ga):** subject marker.

- たくさん **(takusan):** many/a lot.

- います **(imasu):** to exist (for living things); polite form.

友達と一緒に見ます。

- **Japanese:** 友達と一緒に見ます。

- **Romaji:** Tomodachi to issho ni mimasu.

- **English:** He watches with his friends.

Grammar and Vocabulary:

- 友達と一緒に **(tomodachi to issho ni):** together with friends.

- 見ます **(mimasu):** to watch/see; polite form.

素晴らしい夜でした。

- **Japanese:** 素晴らしい夜でした。

- **Romaji:** Subarashii yoru deshita.

- **English:** It was a wonderful night.

Grammar and Vocabulary:

- 素晴らしい **(subarashii):** wonderful; "i" adjective.

- 夜 **(yoru):** night.

- でした **(deshita):** past polite form of "です" (desu).

Story 38: 日本語の授業 (Japanese Class)

Story in Japanese

ジョンさんは日本語のクラスに行きます。

先生は親切です。

新しい言葉を学びます。

クラスメートと会話をします。

日本語が上手になります。

勉強が楽しいです。

Comprehension Question

- ジョンさんはクラスで何を学びますか？
  (What does John learn in class?)

Story with Line-by-Line Breakdown

ジョンさんは日本語のクラスに行きます。

- **Japanese:** ジョンさんは日本語のクラスに行きます。

- **Romaji:** Jon-san wa Nihongo no kurasu ni ikimasu.

- **English:** John goes to a Japanese class.

Grammar and Vocabulary:

- 日本語のクラス **(Nihongo no kurasu):** Japanese class; "の" indicates possession.

- に **(ni):** indicates destination.

- 行きます **(ikimasu):** to go; polite form.

先生は親切です。

- **Japanese:** 先生は親切です。

- **Romaji:** Sensei wa shinsetsu desu.

- **English:** The teacher is kind.

Grammar and Vocabulary:

- 先生 **(sensei):** teacher.

- は **(wa):** topic marker.

- 親切 **(shinsetsu):** kind; "na" adjective.

- です **(desu):** polite sentence ending.

新しい言葉を学びます。

- **Japanese:** 新しい言葉を学びます。

- **Romaji:** Atarashii kotoba o manabimasu.

- **English:** He learns new words.

Grammar and Vocabulary:

- 新しい **(atarashii):** new; "i" adjective.

- 言葉 **(kotoba):** words/vocabulary.

- を **(o):** object marker.

- 学びます **(manabimasu):** to learn; polite form.

クラスメートと会話をします。

- **Japanese:** クラスメートと会話をします。

- **Romaji:** Kurasumeeto to kaiwa o shimasu.

- **English:** He has conversations with classmates.

Grammar and Vocabulary:

- クラスメート **(kurasumeeto):** classmate.

- と **(to):** with.

- 会話 **(kaiwa):** conversation.

- をします **(o shimasu):** to do; polite form.

日本語が上手になります。

- **Japanese:** 日本語が上手になります。

- **Romaji:** Nihongo ga jouzu ni narimasu.

- **English:** His Japanese improves.

Grammar and Vocabulary:

- 日本語 **(Nihongo):** Japanese language.

- が **(ga):** subject marker.

- 上手になる **(jouzu ni naru):** to become skilled/good at.

- なります **(narimasu):** to become; polite form.

勉強が楽しいです。

- **Japanese:** 勉強が楽しいです。

- **Romaji:** Benkyou ga tanoshii desu.

- **English:** Studying is fun.

Grammar and Vocabulary:

- 勉強 **(benkyou):** studying.

- が **(ga):** subject marker.

- 楽しい **(tanoshii):** fun/enjoyable; "i" adjective.

- です **(desu):** polite sentence ending.

Story 39: 日本の映画を見る (Watching a Japanese Movie)

Story in Japanese

ジョンさんは映画館で日本の映画を見ます。

字幕があります。

ストーリーが面白いです。

日本の文化を学びます。

映画の後、友達と感想を話します。

良い映画でした。

Comprehension Question

- ジョンさんはどこで映画を見ますか？
  (Where does John watch the movie?)

Story with Line-by-Line Breakdown

ジョンさんは映画館で日本の映画を見ます。

- **Japanese:** ジョンさんは映画館で日本の映画を見ます。

- **Romaji:** Jon-san wa eigakan de Nihon no eiga o mimasu.

- **English:** John watches a Japanese movie at the cinema.

Grammar and Vocabulary:

- 映画館 **(eigakan):** movie theater/cinema.

- で **(de):** indicates location.

- 日本の映画 **(Nihon no eiga):** Japanese movie; "の" indicates possession.

- を **(o):** object marker.

- 見ます **(mimasu):** to watch; polite form.

字幕があります。

- **Japanese:** 字幕があります。

- **Romaji:** Jimaku ga arimasu.

- **English:** There are subtitles.

Grammar and Vocabulary:

- 字幕 **(jimaku):** subtitles.

- が **(ga):** subject marker.

- あります **(arimasu):** to exist; used for non-living things, polite form.

ストーリーが面白いです。

- **Japanese:** ストーリーが面白いです。

- **Romaji:** Sutoorii ga omoshiroi desu.

- **English:** The story is interesting.

Grammar and Vocabulary:

- ストーリー **(sutoorii):** story.

- が **(ga):** subject marker.

- 面白い **(omoshiroi):** interesting; "i" adjective.

- です **(desu):** polite sentence ending.

日本の文化を学びます。

- **Japanese:** 日本の文化を学びます。

- **Romaji:** Nihon no bunka o manabimasu.

- **English:** He learns about Japanese culture.

Grammar and Vocabulary:

- 日本の文化 **(Nihon no bunka):** Japanese culture; "の" indicates possession.

- を **(o):** object marker.

- 学びます **(manabimasu):** to learn; polite form.

映画の後、友達と感想を話します。

- **Japanese:** 映画の後、友達と感想を話します。

- **Romaji:** Eiga no ato, tomodachi to kansou o hanashimasu.

- **English:** After the movie, he shares his thoughts with his friend.

Grammar and Vocabulary:

- 映画の後 **(eiga no ato):** after the movie.

- 友達と **(tomodachi to):** with a friend.

- 感想 **(kansou):** thoughts/impressions.

- を **(o):** object marker.

- 話します **(hanashimasu):** to talk; polite form.

良い映画でした。

- **Japanese:** 良い映画でした。

- **Romaji:** Yoi eiga deshita.

- **English:** It was a good movie.

Grammar and Vocabulary:

- 良い **(yoi):** good; "i" adjective.

- 映画 **(eiga):** movie.

- でした **(deshita):** past polite form of "です" (desu).

Story 40: 旅の終わり (The End of the Trip)

Story in Japanese

ジョンさんの日本での旅が終わります。

たくさんの思い出があります。

日本の友達にお別れを言います。

「また来ます」と約束します。

空港で飛行機に乗ります。

日本での時間は素晴らしかったです。

Comprehension Question

- ジョンさんは日本での旅の最後に何をしますか？
  (What does John do at the end of his trip to Japan?)

Story with Line-by-Line Breakdown

ジョンさんの日本での旅が終わります。

- **Japanese:** ジョンさんの日本での旅が終わります。

- **Romaji:** Jon-san no Nihon de no tabi ga owarimasu.

- **English:** John's trip in Japan comes to an end.

Grammar and Vocabulary:

- 日本での旅 **(Nihon de no tabi):** trip in Japan; "での" indicates location associated with "trip."

- が **(ga):** subject marker.

- 終わります **(owarimasu):** to end; polite form.

たくさんの思い出があります。

- **Japanese:** たくさんの思い出があります。

- **Romaji:** Takusan no omoide ga arimasu.

- **English:** He has many memories.

Grammar and Vocabulary:

- たくさんの **(takusan no):** many/lots of.

- 思い出 **(omoide):** memories.

- が **(ga):** subject marker.

- あります **(arimasu):** to have/exist (used for non-living things); polite form.

日本の友達にお別れを言います。

- **Japanese:** 日本の友達にお別れを言います。

- **Romaji:** Nihon no tomodachi ni owakare o iimasu.

- **English:** He says goodbye to his Japanese friends.

Grammar and Vocabulary:

- 日本の友達 **(Nihon no tomodachi):** Japanese friends; "の" indicates possession.

- に **(ni):** indicates the person to whom he is saying goodbye.

- お別れ **(owakare):** farewell/goodbye.

- を **(o):** object marker.

- 言います **(iimasu):** to say; polite form.

「また来ます」と約束します。

- **Japanese:** 「また来ます」と約束します。

- **Romaji:** "Mata kimasu" to yakusoku shimasu.

- **English:** He promises, "I will come again."

Grammar and Vocabulary:

- また来ます **(mata kimasu):** I will come again.

- と **(to):** quotation marker.

- 約束します **(yakusoku shimasu):** to promise; polite form.

空港で飛行機に乗ります。

- **Japanese:** 空港で飛行機に乗ります。

- **Romaji:** Kuukou de hikouki ni norimasu.

- **English:** He boards a plane at the airport.

Grammar and Vocabulary:

- 空港 **(kuukou):** airport.

- で **(de):** indicates location of action.

- 飛行機 **(hikouki):** airplane.

- に **(ni):** indicates the vehicle being boarded.

- 乗ります **(norimasu):** to board/ride; polite form.

日本での時間は素晴らしかったです。

- **Japanese:** 日本での時間は素晴らしかったです。

- **Romaji:** Nihon de no jikan wa subarashikatta desu.

- **English:** The time in Japan was wonderful.

Grammar and Vocabulary:

- 日本での時間 **(Nihon de no jikan):** time in Japan; "での" connects location and experience.

- は **(wa):** topic marker.

- 素晴らしかった **(subarashikatta):** wonderful (past form of "subarashii").

- です **(desu):** polite sentence ending.

Story 41: 日本の朝市 (Japanese Morning Market)

Story in Japanese

ジョンさんは朝早く起きます。

ホテルの近くに朝市があります。

たくさんの人が新鮮な野菜や魚を売っています。

ジョンさんはトマトとリンゴを買います。

店の人は「ありがとう」と言います。

ジョンさんは日本語で「どういたしまして」と答えます。

朝市の雰囲気はにぎやかです。

新鮮な食べ物は美味しそうです。

ジョンさんは公園で買ったリンゴを食べます。

とても美味しくて満足です。

Comprehension Question

- ジョンさんは朝市で何を買いますか？
  (What does John buy at the morning market?)

Story with Line-by-Line Breakdown

ジョンさんは朝早く起きます。

- **Japanese:** ジョンさんは朝早く起きます。

- **Romaji:** Jon-san wa asa hayaku okimasu.

- **English:** John wakes up early in the morning.

Grammar and Vocabulary:

- 朝早く **(asa hayaku):** early in the morning.

- 起きます **(okimasu):** to wake up; polite form.

ホテルの近くに朝市があります。

- **Japanese:** ホテルの近くに朝市があります。

- **Romaji:** Hoteru no chikaku ni asaichi ga arimasu.

- **English:** There is a morning market near the hotel.

Grammar and Vocabulary:

- ホテルの近く **(hoteru no chikaku):** near the hotel; "の" indicates possession/location.

- 朝市 **(asaichi):** morning market.

- があります **(ga arimasu):** to exist; used for non-living things, polite form.

たくさんの人が新鮮な野菜や魚を売っています。

- **Japanese:** たくさんの人が新鮮な野菜や魚を売っています。

- **Romaji:** Takusan no hito ga shinsen na yasai ya sakana o utteimasu.

- **English:** Many people are selling fresh vegetables and fish.

Grammar and Vocabulary:

- たくさんの人 **(takusan no hito):** many people.

- 新鮮な **(shinsen na):** fresh; "na" adjective.

- 野菜や魚 **(yasai ya sakana):** vegetables and fish; "や" is used to list examples.

- を **(o):** object marker.

- 売っています **(utteimasu):** selling; polite continuous form.

ジョンさんはトマトとリンゴを買います。

- **Japanese:** ジョンさんはトマトとリンゴを買います。

- **Romaji:** Jon-san wa tomato to ringo o kaimasu.

- **English:** John buys tomatoes and an apple.

Grammar and Vocabulary:

- トマトとリンゴ **(tomato to ringo):** tomatoes and an apple.

- を **(o):** object marker.

- 買います **(kaimasu):** to buy; polite form.

店の人は「ありがとう」と言います。

- **Japanese:** 店の人は「ありがとう」と言います。

- **Romaji:** Mise no hito wa "arigatou" to iimasu.

- **English:** The shopkeeper says, "Thank you."

Grammar and Vocabulary:

- 店の人 **(mise no hito):** shopkeeper (literally "person of the shop").

- は **(wa):** topic marker.

- ありがとう **(arigatou):** thank you (casual form).

- と言います **(to iimasu):** to say (indirect quote marker "と" + "言います" to say).

ジョンさんは日本語で「どういたしまして」と答えます。

- **Japanese:** ジョンさんは日本語で「どういたしまして」と答えます。

- **Romaji:** Jon-san wa Nihongo de "douitashimashite" to kotaemasu.

- **English:** John replies in Japanese, "You're welcome."

Grammar and Vocabulary:

- 日本語で **(Nihongo de):** in Japanese.

- どういたしまして **(douitashimashite):** you're welcome.

- と答えます **(to kotaemasu):** to reply (quoting "と" + "答えます" to reply).

朝市の雰囲気はにぎやかです。

- **Japanese:** 朝市の雰囲気はにぎやかです。

- **Romaji:** Asaichi no fun'iki wa nigiyaka desu.

- **English:** The atmosphere of the morning market is lively.

Grammar and Vocabulary:

- 朝市の雰囲気 **(asaichi no fun'iki):** atmosphere of the morning market.

- は **(wa):** topic marker.

- にぎやか **(nigiyaka):** lively; "na" adjective.

- です **(desu):** polite sentence ending.

新鮮な食べ物は美味しそうです。

- **Japanese:** 新鮮な食べ物は美味しそうです。

- **Romaji:** Shinsen na tabemono wa oishisou desu.

- **English:** The fresh food looks delicious.

Grammar and Vocabulary:

- 新鮮な食べ物 **(shinsen na tabemono):** fresh food.

- は **(wa):** topic marker.

- 美味しそう **(oishisou):** looks delicious; "そう" indicates appearance or assumption.

- です **(desu):** polite sentence ending.

ジョンさんは公園で買ったリンゴを食べます。

- **Japanese:** ジョンさんは公園で買ったリンゴを食べます。

- **Romaji:** Jon-san wa kouen de katta ringo o tabemasu.

- **English:** John eats the apple he bought in the park.

Grammar and Vocabulary:

- 公園で **(kouen de):** at the park.

- 買ったリンゴ **(katta ringo):** the apple he bought; "買った" is the past form of "買う" (to buy), used to modify "リンゴ."

- を **(o):** object marker.

- 食べます **(tabemasu):** to eat; polite form.

とても美味しくて満足です。

- **Japanese:** とても美味しくて満足です。

- **Romaji:** Totemo oishikute manzoku desu.

- **English:** It's very delicious, and he's satisfied.

Grammar and Vocabulary:

- とても **(totemo):** very.

- 美味しくて **(oishikute):** delicious; "て" form to connect adjectives.

- 満足 **(manzoku):** satisfaction/contentment.

- です **(desu):** polite sentence ending.

Story 42: 日本の喫茶店 (Japanese Café)

Story in Japanese

ジョンさんは喫茶店に入ります。

静かな音楽が流れています。

店員さんが「いらっしゃいませ」と言います。

ジョンさんはコーヒーを注文します。

席に座って、店の中を見渡します。

日本の喫茶店は落ち着いた雰囲気です。

コーヒーが運ばれてきます。

ジョンさんはコーヒーを飲みながら本を読みます。

時間がゆっくり流れます。

リラックスできて、良い時間を過ごしました。

Comprehension Question

- ジョンさんは喫茶店で何を飲みますか？
  (What does John drink at the café?)

Story with Line-by-Line Breakdown

ジョンさんは喫茶店に入ります。

- **Japanese:** ジョンさんは喫茶店に入ります。

- **Romaji:** Jon-san wa kissaten ni hairimasu.

- **English:** John enters the café.

Grammar and Vocabulary:

- 喫茶店 **(kissaten):** café.

- に **(ni):** indicates the destination.

- 入ります **(hairimasu):** to enter; polite form.

静かな音楽が流れています。

- **Japanese:** 静かな音楽が流れています。

- **Romaji:** Shizuka na ongaku ga nagareteimasu.

- **English:** Quiet music is playing.

Grammar and Vocabulary:

- 静かな **(shizuka na):** quiet; "na" adjective.

- 音楽 **(ongaku):** music.

- が **(ga):** subject marker.

- 流れています **(nagareteimasu):** is playing/flowing; polite continuous form.

店員さんが「いらっしゃいませ」と言います。

- **Japanese:** 店員さんが「いらっしゃいませ」と言います。

- **Romaji:** Ten'in-san ga "irasshaimase" to iimasu.

- **English:** The staff says, "Welcome."

Grammar and Vocabulary:

- 店員さん **(ten'in-san):** staff member; "さん" is an honorific.

- が **(ga):** subject marker.

- いらっしゃいませ **(irasshaimase):** welcome (formal greeting in stores).

- と言います **(to iimasu):** to say (indirect quote marker "と" + "言います" to say).

ジョンさんはコーヒーを注文します。

- **Japanese:** ジョンさんはコーヒーを注文します。

- **Romaji:** Jon-san wa koohii o chuumon shimasu.

- **English:** John orders coffee.

Grammar and Vocabulary:

- コーヒー **(koohii):** coffee.

- を **(o):** object marker.

- 注文します **(chuumon shimasu):** to order; polite form.

席に座って、店の中を見渡します。

- **Japanese:** 席に座って、店の中を見渡します。

- **Romaji:** Seki ni suwatte, mise no naka o miwatashimasu.

- **English:** He sits at a seat and looks around the café.

Grammar and Vocabulary:

- 席 **(seki):** seat.

- に **(ni):** indicates location.

- 座って **(suwatte):** sitting (te-form of "suwaru" to connect actions).

- 店の中 **(mise no naka):** inside the café.

- を **(o):** object marker.

- 見渡します **(miwatashimasu):** to look around; polite form.

日本の喫茶店は落ち着いた雰囲気です。

- **Japanese:** 日本の喫茶店は落ち着いた雰囲気です。

- **Romaji:** Nihon no kissaten wa ochitsuita fun'iki desu.

- **English:** Japanese cafés have a calm atmosphere.

Grammar and Vocabulary:

- 日本の喫茶店 (**Nihon no kissaten**): Japanese café; "の" indicates possession.

- 落ち着いた (**ochitsuita**): calm/relaxed; adjective form.

- 雰囲気 (**fun'iki**): atmosphere.

- です (**desu**): polite sentence ending.

コーヒーが運ばれてきます。

- **Japanese:** コーヒーが運ばれてきます。

- **Romaji:** Koohii ga hakobarete kimasu.

- **English:** The coffee is brought over.

Grammar and Vocabulary:

- コーヒー (**koohii**): coffee.

- が (**ga**): subject marker.

- 運ばれてきます (**hakobarete kimasu**): to be brought over; polite form.

ジョンさんはコーヒーを飲みながら本を読みます。

- **Japanese:** ジョンさんはコーヒーを飲みながら本を読みます。

- **Romaji:** Jon-san wa koohii o nominagara hon o yomimasu.

- **English:** John drinks coffee while reading a book.

Grammar and Vocabulary:

- 飲みながら (**nominagara**): while drinking (expresses doing two things at the same time).

- 本 (**hon**): book.

- を (**o**): object marker.

- 読みます (**yomimasu**): to read; polite form.

時間がゆっくり流れます。

- **Japanese:** 時間がゆっくり流れます。

- **Romaji:** Jikan ga yukkuri nagaremasu.

- **English:** Time flows slowly.

Grammar and Vocabulary:

- 時間 **(jikan):** time.

- が **(ga):** subject marker.

- ゆっくり **(yukkuri):** slowly.

- 流れます **(nagaremasu):** to flow; polite form.

リラックスできて、良い時間を過ごしました。

- **Japanese:** リラックスできて、良い時間を過ごしました。

- **Romaji:** Rirakkusu dekite, yoi jikan o sugoshimashita.

- **English:** He was able to relax and had a good time.

Grammar and Vocabulary:

- リラックスできて **(rirakkusu dekite):** was able to relax (te-form connecting phrases).

- 良い時間 **(yoi jikan):** good time.

- を **(o):** object marker.

- 過ごしました **(sugoshimashita):** spent (past polite form of "sugosu" - to spend time).

Story 43: 日本の郵便局 (Japanese Post Office)

Story in Japanese

ジョンさんは郵便局に行きます。

家族にハガキを送りたいです。

郵便局で切手を買います。

「アメリカまでいくらですか？」と聞きます。

店員さんは「七十円です」と答えます。

ジョンさんは切手をハガキに貼ります。

家族へのメッセージを書きます。

ポストにハガキを入れます。

「無事に届くといいな」と思います。

初めての日本の郵便局の体験でした。

Comprehension Question

- ジョンさんは誰にハガキを送りたいですか？
  (Who does John want to send a postcard to?)

Story with Line-by-Line Breakdown

ジョンさんは郵便局に行きます。

- **Japanese:** ジョンさんは郵便局に行きます。

- **Romaji:** Jon-san wa yuubinkyoku ni ikimasu.

- **English:** John goes to the post office.

Grammar and Vocabulary:

- 郵便局 **(yuubinkyoku):** post office.

- に **(ni):** indicates the destination.

- 行きます **(ikimasu):** to go; polite form.

家族にハガキを送りたいです。

- **Japanese:** 家族にハガキを送りたいです。

- **Romaji:** Kazoku ni hagaki o okuritai desu.

- **English:** He wants to send a postcard to his family.

Grammar and Vocabulary:

- 家族に **(kazoku ni):** to family.

- ハガキ **(hagaki):** postcard.

- を **(o):** object marker.

- 送りたいです **(okuritai desu):** wants to send (using "たい" form to express desire).

郵便局で切手を買います。

- **Japanese:** 郵便局で切手を買います。

- **Romaji:** Yuubinkyoku de kitte o kaimasu.

- **English:** He buys a stamp at the post office.

Grammar and Vocabulary:

- 郵便局で **(yuubinkyoku de):** at the post office.

- 切手 **(kitte):** stamp.

- を **(o):** object marker.

- 買います **(kaimasu):** to buy; polite form.

「アメリカまでいくらですか？」と聞きます。

- **Japanese:** 「アメリカまでいくらですか？」と聞きます。

- **Romaji:** "Amerika made ikura desu ka?" to kikimasu.

- **English:** He asks, "How much is it to America?"

Grammar and Vocabulary:

- アメリカまで **(Amerika made):** to America; "まで" indicates the destination.

- いくらですか？ **(ikura desu ka?):** how much is it?

- と聞きます **(to kikimasu):** to ask (indirect quote marker "と" + "聞きます" to ask).

店員さんは「七十円です」と答えます。

- **Japanese:** 店員さんは「七十円です」と答えます。

- **Romaji:** Ten'in-san wa "nanajuu en desu" to kotaemasu.

- **English:** The clerk replies, "It's seventy yen."

Grammar and Vocabulary:

- 店員さん **(ten'in-san):** clerk/staff; "さん" is an honorific.

- 七十円 **(nanajuu en):** seventy yen.

- です **(desu):** polite sentence ending.

- と答えます **(to kotaemasu):** to reply (indirect quote marker "と" + "答えます" to reply).

ジョンさんは切手をハガキに貼ります。

- **Japanese:** ジョンさんは切手をハガキに貼ります。

- **Romaji:** Jon-san wa kitte o hagaki ni harimasu.

- **English:** John attaches the stamp to the postcard.

Grammar and Vocabulary:

- 切手 **(kitte):** stamp.

- を **(o):** object marker.

- ハガキに **(hagaki ni):** on the postcard; "に" indicates the target location.

- 貼ります **(harimasu):** to attach/stick; polite form.

家族へのメッセージを書きます。

- **Japanese:** 家族へのメッセージを書きます。

- **Romaji:** Kazoku e no messeeji o kakimasu.

- **English:** He writes a message for his family.

Grammar and Vocabulary:

- 家族への **(kazoku e no):** for/to family; "への" indicates the recipient.

- メッセージ **(messeeji):** message.

- を **(o):** object marker.

- 書きます **(kakimasu):** to write; polite form.

ポストにハガキを入れます。

- **Japanese:** ポストにハガキを入れます。

- **Romaji:** Posuto ni hagaki o iremasu.

- **English:** He puts the postcard in the mailbox.

Grammar and Vocabulary:

- ポスト **(posuto):** mailbox/postbox.

- に **(ni):** indicates the destination.

- ハガキ **(hagaki):** postcard.

- を **(o):** object marker.

- 入れます **(iremasu):** to put in; polite form.

「無事に届くといいな」と思います。

- **Japanese:** 「無事に届くといいな」と思います。

- **Romaji:** "Buji ni todoku to ii na" to omoimasu.

- **English:** He thinks, "I hope it arrives safely."

Grammar and Vocabulary:

- 無事に **(buji ni):** safely.

- 届く **(todoku):** to arrive.

- といいな **(to ii na):** I hope (expressing hope or wish).

- と思います **(to omoimasu):** to think (indirect quote marker "と" + "思います" to think).

初めての日本の郵便局の体験でした。

- **Japanese:** 初めての日本の郵便局の体験でした。

- **Romaji:** Hajimete no Nihon no yuubinkyoku no taiken deshita.

- **English:** It was his first experience at a Japanese post office.

Grammar and Vocabulary:

- 初めての **(hajimete no):** first.

- 日本の郵便局 **(Nihon no yuubinkyoku):** Japanese post office.

- 体験 **(taiken):** experience.

- でした **(deshita):** past polite form of "です" (desu).

Story 44: 日本のコンビニ (Japanese Convenience Store)

Story in Japanese

ジョンさんはコンビニに入ります。

24時間開いている便利なお店です。

おにぎりや弁当が売っています。

ジョンさんはおにぎりとお茶を買います。

店員さんは「ポイントカードはお持ちですか？」と聞きます。

ジョンさんは「いいえ、持っていません」と答えます。

支払いをして、レシートをもらいます。

店を出て、公園でおにぎりを食べます。

コンビニのおにぎりは美味しいです。

日本のコンビニはとても便利だと感じます。

Comprehension Question

- ジョンさんはコンビニで何を買いますか？
  (What does John buy at the convenience store?)

Story with Line-by-Line Breakdown

ジョンさんはコンビニに入ります。

- **Japanese:** ジョンさんはコンビニに入ります。

- **Romaji:** Jon-san wa konbini ni hairimasu.

- **English:** John enters the convenience store.

Grammar and Vocabulary:

- コンビニ **(konbini):** convenience store.

- に **(ni):** indicates the destination.

- 入ります **(hairimasu):** to enter; polite form.

24時間開いている便利なお店です。

- **Japanese:** 24時間開いている便利なお店です。

- **Romaji:** Nijuu yo jikan aiteiru benri na omise desu.

- **English:** It's a convenient store that is open 24 hours.

Grammar and Vocabulary:

- 24時間 **(nijuu yo jikan):** 24 hours.

- 開いている **(aiteiru):** open; continuous form.

- 便利な **(benri na):** convenient; "na" adjective.

- お店 **(omise):** store.

- です **(desu):** polite sentence ending.

おにぎりや弁当が売っています。

- **Japanese:** おにぎりや弁当が売っています。

- **Romaji:** Onigiri ya bentou ga utteimasu.

- **English:** They sell rice balls and bento boxes.

Grammar and Vocabulary:

- おにぎり **(onigiri):** rice ball.

- 弁当 **(bentou):** bento box (boxed meal).

- や **(ya):** and (used for listing examples).

- が **(ga):** subject marker.

- 売っています **(utteimasu):** selling; polite continuous form.

ジョンさんはおにぎりとお茶を買います。

- **Japanese:** ジョンさんはおにぎりとお茶を買います。

- **Romaji:** Jon-san wa onigiri to ocha o kaimasu.

- **English:** John buys a rice ball and tea.

Grammar and Vocabulary:

- おにぎり **(onigiri):** rice ball.

- と **(to):** and.

- お茶 **(ocha):** tea.

- を **(o):** object marker.

- 買います **(kaimasu):** to buy; polite form.

店員さんは「ポイントカードはお持ちですか？」と聞きます。

- **Japanese:** 店員さんは「ポイントカードはお持ちですか？」と聞きます。

- **Romaji:** Ten'in-san wa "pointo kaado wa omochi desu ka?" to kikimasu.

- **English:** The clerk asks, "Do you have a point card?"

Grammar and Vocabulary:

- 店員さん **(ten'in-san):** clerk/staff; "さん" is an honorific.

- ポイントカード **(pointo kaado):** point card.

- は **(wa):** topic marker.

- お持ちですか？ **(omochi desu ka?):** do you have? (polite form).

- と聞きます **(to kikimasu):** to ask (indirect quote marker "と" + "聞きます" to ask).

ジョンさんは「いいえ、持っていません」と答えます。

- **Japanese:** ジョンさんは「いいえ、持っていません」と答えます。

- **Romaji:** Jon-san wa "iie, motteimasen" to kotaemasu.

- **English:** John replies, "No, I don't have one."

Grammar and Vocabulary:

- いいえ **(iie):** no.

- 持っていません **(motteimasen):** don't have; polite negative form.

- と答えます **(to kotaemasu):** to reply (indirect quote marker "と" + "答えます" to reply).

支払いをして、レシートをもらいます。

- **Japanese:** 支払いをして、レシートをもらいます。

- **Romaji:** Shiharai o shite, reshiito o moraimasu.

- **English:** He makes the payment and receives the receipt.

Grammar and Vocabulary:

- 支払い **(shiharai):** payment.

- をして **(o shite):** to do (payment); te-form to connect actions.

- レシート **(reshiito):** receipt.

- をもらいます **(o moraimasu):** to receive; polite form.

店を出て、公園でおにぎりを食べます。

- **Japanese:** 店を出て、公園でおにぎりを食べます。

- **Romaji:** Mise o dete, kouen de onigiri o tabemasu.

- **English:** He leaves the store and eats the rice ball at the park.

Grammar and Vocabulary:

- 店を出て **(mise o dete):** leaves the store (te-form connecting actions).

- 公園で **(kouen de):** at the park.

- おにぎり **(onigiri):** rice ball.

- を食べます **(o tabemasu):** to eat; polite form.

コンビニのおにぎりは美味しいです。

- **Japanese:** コンビニのおにぎりは美味しいです。

- **Romaji:** Konbini no onigiri wa oishii desu.

- **English:** The convenience store rice ball is delicious.

Grammar and Vocabulary:

- コンビニのおにぎり **(konbini no onigiri):** convenience store rice ball; "の" indicates possession.

- は **(wa):** topic marker.

- 美味しい **(oishii):** delicious; "i" adjective.

- です **(desu):** polite sentence ending.

日本のコンビニはとても便利だと感じます。

- **Japanese:** 日本のコンビニはとても便利だと感じます。

- **Romaji:** Nihon no konbini wa totemo benri da to kanjimasu.

- **English:** He feels that Japanese convenience stores are very convenient.

Grammar and Vocabulary:

- 日本のコンビニ **(Nihon no konbini):** Japanese convenience store.

- は **(wa):** topic marker.

- とても **(totemo):** very.

- 便利 **(benri):** convenient; "na" adjective.

- だと感じます **(da to kanjimasu):** feels that (using "だと" to indicate an impression or feeling).

Story 46: 日本の雨の日 (A Rainy Day in Japan)

Story in Japanese

今日は雨が降っています。

ジョンさんは傘を持って出かけます。

雨の日の日本の街も美しいです。

道に映る光がきれいです。

ジョンさんは美術館に行くことにします。

美術館の中は静かです。

たくさんの絵や彫刻があります。

雨の音が聞こえて、心が落ち着きます。

外に出ると、雨は止んでいました。

雨の日も楽しい一日でした。

Comprehension Question

ジョンさんは雨の日にどこへ行きますか？
(Where does John decide to go on a rainy day?)

Story with Line-by-Line Breakdown

今日は雨が降っています。

- **Japanese:** 今日は雨が降っています。

- **Romaji:** Kyou wa ame ga futteimasu.

- **English:** It is raining today.

Grammar and Vocabulary:

- 今日 **(kyou):** Today.

- は **(wa):** Topic marker.

- 雨 **(ame):** Rain.

- が **(ga):** Subject marker.

- 降っています **(futteimasu):** Is raining; polite continuous form of "降る" (furu).

ジョンさんは傘を持って出かけます。

- **Japanese:** ジョンさんは傘を持って出かけます。

- **Romaji:** Jon-san wa kasa o motte dekakemasu.

- **English:** John goes out carrying an umbrella.

Grammar and Vocabulary:

- ジョンさん **(Jon-san):** John; "さん" is an honorific suffix.

- は **(wa):** Topic marker.

- 傘 **(kasa):** Umbrella.

- を **(o):** Object marker.

- 持って **(motte):** Carrying; te-form of "持つ" (motsu).

- 出かけます **(dekakemasu):** To go out; polite form.

雨の日の日本の街も美しいです。

- **Japanese:** 雨の日の日本の街も美しいです。

- **Romaji:** Ame no hi no Nihon no machi mo utsukushii desu.

- **English:** Even on rainy days, Japanese streets are beautiful.

Grammar and Vocabulary:

- 雨の日 **(ame no hi):** Rainy day.

    o の **(no):** Possessive particle.

    o 日本の **(Nihon no):** Japanese; "の" indicates possession.

    o 街 **(machi):** Town, street.

    o も **(mo):** Also, too.

    o 美しい **(utsukushii):** Beautiful; "i" adjective.

    o です **(desu):** Polite sentence ending.

道に映る光がきれいです。

- **Japanese:** 道に映る光がきれいです。

- **Romaji:** Michi ni utsuru hikari ga kirei desu.

- **English:** The lights reflecting on the street are beautiful.

Grammar and Vocabulary:

- 道 **(michi):** Street, road.

- に **(ni):** Location marker.

- 映る **(utsuru):** To reflect.

- 光 **(hikari):** Light.

- が **(ga):** Subject marker.

- きれい **(kirei)**: Beautiful, clean.

- です **(desu)**: Polite sentence ending.

ジョンさんは美術館に行くことにします。

- **Japanese:** ジョンさんは美術館に行くことにします。

- **Romaji:** Jon-san wa bijutsukan ni iku koto ni shimasu.

- **English:** John decides to go to the art museum.

Grammar and Vocabulary:

- ジョンさん **(Jon-san)**: John.

- は **(wa)**: Topic marker.

- 美術館 **(bijutsukan)**: Art museum.

- に **(ni)**: Direction or location marker.

- 行く **(iku)**: To go.

- ことにします **(koto ni shimasu)**: Decides to do; "ことにする" expresses a decision.

美術館の中は静かです。

- **Japanese:** 美術館の中は静かです。

- **Romaji:** Bijutsukan no naka wa shizuka desu.

- **English:** It is quiet inside the art museum.

Grammar and Vocabulary:

- 美術館 **(bijutsukan)**: Art museum.

- の **(no)**: Possessive particle.

- 中 **(naka)**: Inside.

- は **(wa)**: Topic marker.

- 静か **(shizuka):** Quiet; "na" adjective.

- です **(desu):** Polite sentence ending.

たくさんの絵や彫刻があります。

- **Japanese:** たくさんの絵や彫刻があります。

- **Romaji:** Takusan no e ya choukoku ga arimasu.

- **English:** There are many paintings and sculptures.

Grammar and Vocabulary:

- たくさん **(takusan):** Many, a lot.

- の **(no):** Possessive particle.

- 絵 **(e):** Painting.

- や **(ya):** And; used to list examples.

- 彫刻 **(choukoku):** Sculpture.

- が **(ga):** Subject marker.

- あります **(arimasu):** There are; polite form.

雨の音が聞こえて、心が落ち着きます。

- **Japanese:** 雨の音が聞こえて、心が落ち着きます。

- **Romaji:** Ame no oto ga kikoete, kokoro ga ochitsukimasu.

- **English:** He hears the sound of rain and feels calm.

Grammar and Vocabulary:

- 雨 **(ame):** Rain.

- の **(no):** Possessive particle.

- 音 **(oto):** Sound.

- が **(ga):** Subject marker.

- 聞こえて **(kikoete):** Hearing; te-form of "聞こえる" (kikoeru).

- 心 **(kokoro):** Heart, mind.

- が **(ga):** Subject marker.

- 落ち着きます **(ochitsukimasu):** To calm down; polite form.

外に出ると、雨は止んでいました。

- **Japanese:** 外に出ると、雨は止んでいました。

- **Romaji:** Soto ni deru to, ame wa yandeimashita.

- **English:** When he went outside, the rain had stopped.

Grammar and Vocabulary:

- 外 **(soto):** Outside.

- に **(ni):** Direction or location marker.

- 出る **(deru):** To go out.

- と **(to):** When (conditional).

- 雨 **(ame):** Rain.

- は **(wa):** Topic marker.

- 止んでいました **(yandeimashita):** Had stopped; past progressive form of "止む" (yamu).

雨の日も楽しい一日でした。

- **Japanese:** 雨の日も楽しい一日でした。

- **Romaji:** Ame no hi mo tanoshii ichinichi deshita.

- **English:** It was a fun day even on a rainy day.

Grammar and Vocabulary:

- 雨の日 **(ame no hi):** Rainy day.

- も **(mo):** Also, even.

- 楽しい **(tanoshii):** Fun, enjoyable; "i" adjective.

- 一日 **(ichinichi):** One day.

- でした **(deshita):** Was; past polite form of "です" (desu).

Story 47: 友達の家で料理 (Cooking at a Friend's House)

ジョンさんは日本人の友達の家に招かれます。

一緒に料理を作ります。

今日はカレーライスを作ります。

野菜や肉を切ります。

鍋で材料を炒めます。

カレールーを入れて煮込みます。

ご飯が炊けました。

みんなで「いただきます」と言って食べます。

とても美味しいです。

楽しい時間を過ごしました。

Comprehension Question

ジョンさんたちは何を作りますか？
(What do John and his friends cook together?)

Story with Line-by-Line Breakdown

ジョンさんは日本人の友達の家に招かれます。

- **Japanese:** ジョンさんは日本人の友達の家に招かれます。

- **Romaji:** Jon-san wa Nihonjin no tomodachi no ie ni manekaremasu.

- **English:** John is invited to his Japanese friend's house.

Grammar and Vocabulary:

- ジョンさん **(Jon-san):** John.

- は **(wa):** Topic marker.

- 日本人 **(Nihonjin):** Japanese person.

- の **(no):** Possessive particle.

- 友達 **(tomodachi):** Friend.

- 家 **(ie):** House.

- に **(ni):** Direction or location marker.

- 招かれます **(manekaremasu):** Is invited; passive form of "招く" (maneku).

一緒に料理を作ります。

- **Japanese:** 一緒に料理を作ります。

- **Romaji:** Issho ni ryouri o tsukurimasu.

- **English:** They cook together.

Grammar and Vocabulary:

- 一緒に **(issho ni):** Together.

- 料理 **(ryouri):** Cooking, meal.

- を **(o):** Object marker.

- 作ります **(tsukurimasu):** To make, to cook; polite form.

今日はカレーライスを作ります。

- **Japanese:** 今日はカレーライスを作ります。

- **Romaji:** Kyou wa karee raisu o tsukurimasu.

- **English:** Today, they will make curry rice.

Grammar and Vocabulary:

- 今日 **(kyou):** Today.

- は **(wa):** Topic marker.

- カレーライス **(karee raisu):** Curry rice.

- を **(o):** Object marker.

- 作ります **(tsukurimasu):** To make, to cook; polite form.

野菜や肉を切ります。

- **Japanese:** 野菜や肉を切ります。

- **Romaji:** Yasai ya niku o kirimasu.

- **English:** They cut vegetables and meat.

Grammar and Vocabulary:

- 野菜 **(yasai):** Vegetables.

- や **(ya):** And; used to list examples.

- 肉 **(niku):** Meat.

- を **(o):** Object marker.

- 切ります **(kirimasu):** To cut; polite form.

鍋で材料を炒めます。

- **Japanese:** 鍋で材料を炒めます。

- **Romaji:** Nabe de zairyou o itamemasu.

- **English:** They stir-fry the ingredients in a pot.

Grammar and Vocabulary:

- 鍋 **(nabe):** Pot.

- で **(de):** Indicates the means or location of an action.

- 材料 **(zairyou):** Ingredients.

- を **(o):** Object marker.

- 炒めます **(itamemasu):** To stir-fry; polite form.

カレールーを入れて煮込みます。

- **Japanese:** カレールーを入れて煮込みます。

- **Romaji:** Karee ruu o irete nikomimasu.

- **English:** They add curry roux and let it simmer.

Grammar and Vocabulary:

- カレールー **(karee ruu):** Curry roux.

- を **(o):** Object marker.

- 入れて **(irete):** Adding; te-form of "入れる" (ireru).

- 煮込みます **(nikomimasu):** To simmer, stew; polite form.

ご飯が炊けました。

- **Japanese:** ご飯が炊けました。

- **Romaji:** Gohan ga takemashita.

- **English:** The rice is cooked.

Grammar and Vocabulary:

- ご飯 **(gohan):** Cooked rice, meal.

- が **(ga):** Subject marker.

- 炊けました **(takemashita):** Was cooked; past polite form of "炊く" (taku).

みんなで「いただきます」と言って食べます。

- **Japanese:** みんなで「いただきます」と言って食べます。

- **Romaji:** Minna de "itadakimasu" to itte tabemasu.

- **English:** Everyone says "itadakimasu" and eats together.

Grammar and Vocabulary:

- みんなで **(minna de):** Everyone together.

- 「いただきます」 **(itadakimasu):** A phrase said before eating, expressing gratitude.

- と **(to):** Quotation particle.

- 言って **(itte):** Saying; te-form of "言う" (iu).

- 食べます **(tabemasu):** To eat; polite form.

とても美味しいです。

- **Japanese:** とても美味しいです。

- **Romaji:** Totemo oishii desu.

- **English:** It is very delicious.

Grammar and Vocabulary:

- とても **(totemo):** Very.

- 美味しい **(oishii):** Delicious; "i" adjective.

- です **(desu):** Polite sentence ending.

楽しい時間を過ごしました。

- **Japanese:** 楽しい時間を過ごしました。

- **Romaji:** Tanoshii jikan o sugoshimashita.

- **English:** They spent a fun time.

Grammar and Vocabulary:

- 楽しい **(tanoshii):** Fun, enjoyable; "i" adjective.

- 時間 **(jikan):** Time.

- を **(o):** Object marker.

- 過ごしました **(sugoshimashita):** Spent; past polite form of "過ごす" (sugosu).

Story 48: 日本の夜景 (Night View of Japan)

Story in Japanese

ジョンさんは夜、展望台に行きます。

高いビルからの景色は素晴らしいです。

街の明かりがきらきら光っています。

ジョンさんは写真を撮ります。

風が少し冷たいです。

ベンチに座って夜景を眺めます。

静かな時間が流れます。

日本の夜は美しいと感じます。

友達に夜景の写真を送ります。

良い思い出になりました。

Comprehension Question

ジョンさんは夜に何をしますか？
(What does John do at night?)

Story with Line-by-Line Breakdown

ジョンさんは夜、展望台に行きます。

- **Japanese:** ジョンさんは夜、展望台に行きます。

- **Romaji:** Jon-san wa yoru, tenboudai ni ikimasu.

- **English:** John goes to the observatory at night.

Grammar and Vocabulary:

- ジョンさん **(Jon-san):** John.

- は **(wa):** Topic marker.

- 夜 **(yoru):** Night.

- 、 **(、):** Comma, indicating a pause.

- 展望台 **(tenboudai):** Observatory, observation deck.

- に **(ni):** Direction or location marker.

- 行きます **(ikimasu):** To go; polite form.

高いビルからの景色は素晴らしいです。

- **Japanese:** 高いビルからの景色は素晴らしいです。

- **Romaji:** Takai biru kara no keshiki wa subarashii desu.

- **English:** The view from the tall building is wonderful.

Grammar and Vocabulary:

- 高い **(takai):** Tall, high.

- ビル **(biru):** Building.

- から **(kara):** From.

- の **(no):** Possessive particle.

- 景色 **(keshiki):** Scenery, view.

- は **(wa):** Topic marker.

- 素晴らしい **(subarashii):** Wonderful; "i" adjective.

- です **(desu):** Polite sentence ending.

街の明かりがきらきら光っています。

- **Japanese:** 街の明かりがきらきら光っています。

- **Romaji:** Machi no akari ga kirakira hikari teimasu.

- **English:** The city lights are sparkling.

Grammar and Vocabulary:

- 街 **(machi):** City, town.

- の **(no):** Possessive particle.

- 明かり **(akari):** Lights.

- が **(ga):** Subject marker.

- きらきら **(kirakira):** Sparkling, glittering; onomatopoeia.

- 光っています **(hikari teimasu):** Are shining; polite continuous form of "光る" (hikaru).

ジョンさんは写真を撮ります。

- **Japanese:** ジョンさんは写真を撮ります。

- **Romaji:** Jon-san wa shashin o torimasu.

- **English:** John takes photos.

Grammar and Vocabulary:

- ジョンさん **(Jon-san):** John.

- は **(wa):** Topic marker.

- 写真 **(shashin):** Photo.

- を **(o):** Object marker.

- 撮ります **(torimasu):** To take (a photo); polite form.

風が少し冷たいです。

- **Japanese:** 風が少し冷たいです。

- **Romaji:** Kaze ga sukoshi tsumetai desu.

- **English:** The wind is a bit cold.

Grammar and Vocabulary:

- 風 **(kaze):** Wind.

- が **(ga):** Subject marker.

- 少し **(sukoshi):** A little, slightly.

- 冷たい **(tsumetai):** Cold (to the touch); "i" adjective.

- です **(desu):** Polite sentence ending.

ベンチに座って夜景を眺めます。

- **Japanese:** ベンチに座って夜景を眺めます。

- **Romaji:** Benchi ni suwatte yakei o nagamemasu.

- **English:** He sits on a bench and gazes at the night view.

Grammar and Vocabulary:

- ベンチ **(benchi):** Bench.

- に **(ni):** Location marker.

- 座って **(suwatte):** Sitting; te-form of "座る" (suwaru).

- 夜景 **(yakei):** Night view, nightscape.

- を **(o):** Object marker.

- 眺めます **(nagamemasu):** To gaze, to look at; polite form.

静かな時間が流れます。

- **Japanese:** 静かな時間が流れます。

- **Romaji:** Shizuka na jikan ga nagaremasu.

- **English:** Quiet time flows by.

Grammar and Vocabulary:

- 静かな **(shizuka na):** Quiet; "na" adjective.

- 時間 **(jikan):** Time.

- が **(ga):** Subject marker.

- 流れます **(nagaremasu):** To flow; polite form.

日本の夜は美しいと感じます。

- **Japanese:** 日本の夜は美しいと感じます。

- **Romaji:** Nihon no yoru wa utsukushii to kanjimasu.

- **English:** He feels that Japanese nights are beautiful.

Grammar and Vocabulary:

- 日本の **(Nihon no):** Japanese; "の" indicates possession.

- 夜 **(yoru):** Night.

- は **(wa):** Topic marker.

- 美しい **(utsukushii):** Beautiful; "i" adjective.

- と **(to):** Quotation particle.

- 感じます **(kanjimasu):** To feel; polite form.

友達に夜景の写真を送ります。

- **Japanese:** 友達に夜景の写真を送ります。

- **Romaji:** Tomodachi ni yakei no shashin o okurimasu.

- **English:** He sends the night view photos to his friends.

Grammar and Vocabulary:

- 友達 **(tomodachi):** Friends.

- に **(ni):** Indirect object marker.

- 夜景 **(yakei):** Night view.

- の **(no):** Possessive particle.

- 写真 **(shashin):** Photo.

- を **(o):** Object marker.

- 送ります **(okurimasu):** To send; polite form.

良い思い出になりました。

- **Japanese:** 良い思い出になりました。

- **Romaji:** Yoi omoide ni narimashita.

- **English:** It became a good memory.

Grammar and Vocabulary:

- 良い **(yoi):** Good.

- 思い出 **(omoide):** Memory.

- に **(ni):** Becomes.

- なりました **(narimashita):** Became; past polite form of "なる" (naru).

Story 49: 日本の文化体験 (Cultural Experience in Japan)

Story in Japanese

ジョンさんは文化センターに行きます。

今日は折り紙を習います。

先生が折り方を教えてくれます。

紙を折って、鶴を作ります。

最初は難しいですが、だんだん上手になります。

色々な形を作ります。

出来上がった作品を持ち帰ります。

とても楽しい体験でした。

日本の文化に触れることができました。

また他の体験もしてみたいです。

Comprehension Question

ジョンさんは文化センターで何を習いますか？
(What does John learn at the cultural center?)

Story with Line-by-Line Breakdown

ジョンさんは文化センターに行きます。

- **Japanese:** ジョンさんは文化センターに行きます。

- **Romaji:** Jon-san wa bunkasentā ni ikimasu.

- **English:** John goes to the cultural center.

- **Grammar and Vocabulary:**

    ○ ジョンさん **(Jon-san):** John; "さん" is an honorific suffix.

- o は **(wa):** Topic marker.

- o 文化センター **(bunkasentā):** Cultural center.

- o に **(ni):** Indicates direction or destination.

- o 行きます **(ikimasu):** To go; polite form.

今日は折り紙を習います。

- **Japanese:** 今日は折り紙を習います。

- **Romaji:** Kyou wa origami o naraimasu.

- **English:** Today, he will learn origami.

Grammar and Vocabulary:

- 今日 **(kyou):** Today.

- は **(wa):** Topic marker.

- 折り紙 **(origami):** Origami (paper folding).

- を **(o):** Object marker.

- 習います **(naraimasu):** To learn; polite form.

先生が折り方を教えてくれます。

- **Japanese:** 先生が折り方を教えてくれます。

- **Romaji:** Sensei ga orikata o oshiete kuremasu.

- **English:** The teacher teaches him how to fold.

Grammar and Vocabulary:

- 先生 **(sensei):** Teacher.

- が **(ga):** Subject marker.

- 折り方 **(orikata):** How to fold; folding method.

- を **(o):** Object marker.

- 教えてくれます **(oshiete kuremasu):** Teaches (with "くれる" indicating a favor).

紙を折って、鶴を作ります。

- **Japanese:** 紙を折って、鶴を作ります。

- **Romaji:** Kami o otte, tsuru o tsukurimasu.

- **English:** He folds the paper and makes a crane.

Grammar and Vocabulary:

- 紙 **(kami):** Paper.

- を **(o):** Object marker.

- 折って **(otte):** Folding; te-form of "折る" (oru).

- 鶴 **(tsuru):** Crane (the bird).

- を作ります **(o tsukurimasu):** To make; polite form.

最初は難しいですが、だんだん上手になります。

- **Japanese:** 最初は難しいですが、だんだん上手になります。

- **Romaji:** Saisho wa muzukashii desu ga, dandan jouzu ni narimasu.

- **English:** It is difficult at first, but he gradually becomes skillful.

Grammar and Vocabulary:

- 最初 **(saisho):** At first, initially.

- は **(wa):** Topic marker.

- 難しい **(muzukashii):** Difficult; "i" adjective.

- ですが **(desu ga):** But; polite form.

- だんだん **(dandan):** Gradually.

- 上手になります **(jouzu ni narimasu):** To become skillful; polite form.

色々な形を作ります。

- **Japanese:** 色々な形を作ります。

- **Romaji:** Iroiro na katachi o tsukurimasu.

- **English:** He makes various shapes.

Grammar and Vocabulary:

- 色々な **(iroiro na):** Various; "na" adjective.

- 形 **(katachi):** Shape, form.

- を作ります **(o tsukurimasu):** To make; polite form.

出来上がった作品を持ち帰ります。

- **Japanese:** 出来上がった作品を持ち帰ります。

- **Romaji:** Dekiagatta sakuhin o mochikaerimasu.

- **English:** He takes the finished works home.

Grammar and Vocabulary:

- 出来上がった **(dekiagatta):** Finished, completed; past form of "出来上がる" (dekiagaru).

- 作品 **(sakuhin):** Work of art, piece.

- を持ち帰ります **(o mochikaerimasu):** To take home; polite form.

とても楽しい体験でした。

- **Japanese:** とても楽しい体験でした。

- **Romaji:** Totemo tanoshii taiken deshita.

- **English:** It was a very enjoyable experience.

Grammar and Vocabulary:

- とても **(totemo):** Very.

- 楽しい **(tanoshii):** Enjoyable, fun; "i" adjective.

- 体験 **(taiken):** Experience.

- でした **(deshita):** Was; past polite form of "です" (desu).

日本の文化に触れることができました。

- **Japanese:** 日本の文化に触れることができました。

- **Romaji:** Nihon no bunka ni fureru koto ga dekimashita.

- **English:** He was able to experience Japanese culture.

Grammar and Vocabulary:

- 日本の **(Nihon no):** Japanese; "の" indicates possession.

- 文化 **(bunka):** Culture.

- に触れる **(ni fureru):** To experience, to touch upon.

- ことができました **(koto ga dekimashita):** Was able to do; past polite form.

また他の体験もしてみたいです。

- **Japanese:** また他の体験もしてみたいです。

- **Romaji:** Mata hoka no taiken mo shite mitai desu.

- **English:** He wants to try other experiences as well.

Grammar and Vocabulary:

- また **(mata):** Also, again.

- 他の **(hoka no):** Other; "no" indicates possession.

- 体験 **(taiken):** Experience.

- も **(mo):** Also, too.

- してみたい **(shite mitai):** Want to try doing.

- です **(desu):** Polite sentence ending.

Story 50: 日本の自転車旅 (Cycling Trip in Japan)

Story in Japanese

ジョンさんは自転車を借ります。

川沿いの道を走ります。

風が気持ちいいです。

途中で休憩して、水を飲みます。

橋を渡って、反対側の道を進みます。

景色がとても綺麗です。

公園に着いて、ベンチに座ります。

自転車での旅は楽しいです。

夕方になり、帰ることにします。

良い運動になりました。

Comprehension Question

ジョンさんは自転車旅で何をしますか？
(What does John do on his cycling trip?)

Story with Line-by-Line Breakdown

ジョンさんは自転車を借ります。

- **Japanese:** ジョンさんは自転車を借ります。

- **Romaji:** Jon-san wa jitensha o karimasu.

- **English:** John rents a bicycle.

Grammar and Vocabulary:

- ジョンさん **(Jon-san):** John; "さん" is an honorific suffix.

- は **(wa):** Topic marker.

- 自転車 **(jitensha):** Bicycle.

- を **(o):** Object marker.

- 借ります **(karimasu):** To rent; polite form.

川沿いの道を走ります。

- **Japanese:** 川沿いの道を走ります。

- **Romaji:** Kawazoi no michi o hashirimasu.

- **English:** He rides along the riverside road.

Grammar and Vocabulary:

- 川沿いの **(kawazoi no):** Riverside; "no" indicates possession.

- 道 **(michi):** Road, path.

- を走ります **(o hashirimasu):** To ride; polite form.

風が気持ちいいです。

- **Japanese:** 風が気持ちいいです。

- **Romaji:** Kaze ga kimochi ii desu.

- **English:** The breeze feels nice.

Grammar and Vocabulary:

- 風 **(kaze):** Breeze, wind.

- が **(ga):** Subject marker.

- 気持ちいい **(kimochi ii):** Feels good, nice.

- です **(desu):** Polite sentence ending.

途中で休憩して、水を飲みます。

- **Japanese:** 途中で休憩して、水を飲みます。

- **Romaji:** Tochuu de kyuukei shite, mizu o nomimasu.

- **English:** He takes a break along the way and drinks water.

Grammar and Vocabulary:

- 途中で **(tochuu de):** Along the way,途中 (tochuu) means "middle,途中で " indicates at the midway point.

- 休憩して **(kyuukei shite):** Taking a break; te-form of "休憩する" (kyuukei suru).

- 水 **(mizu):** Water.

- を飲みます **(o nomimasu):** To drink; polite form.

橋を渡って、反対側の道を進みます。

- **Japanese:** 橋を渡って、反対側の道を進みます。

- **Romaji:** Hashi o watatte, hantai-gawa no michi o susumimasu.

- **English:** He crosses the bridge and proceeds on the road to the opposite side.

Grammar and Vocabulary:

- 橋 **(hashi):** Bridge.

- を渡って **(o watatte):** Crossing; te-form of "渡る" (wataru).

- 反対側の **(hantai-gawa no):** Opposite side; "の" indicates possession.

- 道 **(michi):** Road, path.

- を進みます **(o susumimasu):** To proceed; polite form.

景色がとても綺麗です。

- **Japanese:** 景色がとても綺麗です。

- **Romaji:** Keshiki ga totemo kirei desu.

- **English:** The scenery is very beautiful.

Grammar and Vocabulary:

- 景色 **(keshiki):** Scenery, view.

- が **(ga):** Subject marker.

- とても **(totemo):** Very.

- 綺麗 **(kirei):** Beautiful, clean.

- です **(desu):** Polite sentence ending.

公園に着いて、ベンチに座ります。

- **Japanese:** 公園に着いて、ベンチに座ります。

- **Romaji:** Kouen ni tsuite, benchi ni suwarimasu.

- **English:** He arrives at the park and sits on a bench.

Grammar and Vocabulary:

- 公園 **(kouen):** Park.

- に着いて **(ni tsuite):** Arriving; te-form of "着く" (tsuku).

- ベンチ **(benchi):** Bench.

- に座ります **(ni suwarimasu):** To sit; polite form.

自転車での旅は楽しいです。

- **Japanese:** 自転車での旅は楽しいです。

- **Romaji:** Jitensha de no tabi wa tanoshii desu.

- **English:** A cycling trip is fun.

Grammar and Vocabulary:

- 自転車での **(jitensha de no):** By bicycle; "での" indicates the means.

- 旅 **(tabi):** Trip, journey.

- は **(wa):** Topic marker.

- 楽しい **(tanoshii):** Fun, enjoyable; "i" adjective.

- です **(desu):** Polite sentence ending.

夕方になり、帰ることにします。

- **Japanese:** 夕方になり、帰ることにします。

- **Romaji:** Yuugata ni nari, kaeru koto ni shimasu.

- **English:** In the evening, he decides to go home.

Grammar and Vocabulary:

- 夕方 **(yuugata):** Evening.

- に **(ni):** Time marker.

- なり **(nari):** Becoming; stem form of "なる" (naru).

- 帰ることにします **(kaeru koto ni shimasu):** Decides to go home; "ことにする" expresses a decision.

良い運動になりました。

- **Japanese:** 良い運動になりました。

- **Romaji:** Yoi undou ni narimashita.

- **English:** It became good exercise.

Grammar and Vocabulary:

- 良い **(yoi):** Good.

- 運動 **(undou):** Exercise.

- に **(ni):** Becomes.

- なりました **(narimashita):** Became; past polite form of "なる" (naru).

Story 51: 日本の朝の散歩 (Morning Walk in Japan)

Story in Japanese

ジョンさんは早起きして散歩します。

朝の空気は新鮮です。

公園には犬を連れた人がいます。

桜の木が並んでいます。

花はまだ咲いていませんが、蕾があります。

池には鯉が泳いでいます。

ジョンさんはベンチに座って景色を楽しみます。

鳥の声が聞こえます。

朝の時間は静かで落ち着きます。

一日の良いスタートになりました。

Comprehension Question

ジョンさんの朝の散歩で何を見ますか？
(What does John see during his morning walk?)

Story with Line-by-Line Breakdown

ジョンさんは早起きして散歩します。

- **Japanese:** ジョンさんは早起きして散歩します。

- **Romaji:** Jon-san wa hayaoki shite sanpo shimasu.

- **English:** John wakes up early and goes for a walk.

Grammar and Vocabulary:

- ジョンさん **(Jon-san):** John; "さん" is an honorific suffix.

- は **(wa):** Topic marker.

- 早起きして **(hayaoki shite):** Wakes up early; te-form of "早起きする" (hayaoki suru).

- 散歩します **(sanpo shimasu):** Goes for a walk; polite form.

朝の空気は新鮮です。

- **Japanese:** 朝の空気は新鮮です。

- **Romaji:** Asa no kuuki wa shinsen desu.

- **English:** The morning air is fresh.

Grammar and Vocabulary:

- 朝 **(asa):** Morning.

- の **(no):** Possessive particle.

- 空気 **(kuuki):** Air.

- は **(wa):** Topic marker.

- 新鮮 **(shinsen):** Fresh.

- です **(desu):** Polite sentence ending.

公園には犬を連れた人がいます。

- **Japanese:** 公園には犬を連れた人がいます。

- **Romaji:** Kouen ni wa inu o tsureta hito ga imasu.

- **English:** There are people in the park with dogs.

Grammar and Vocabulary:

- 公園 **(kouen):** Park.

- に **(ni):** Location marker.

- は **(wa):** Topic marker.

- 犬 **(inu):** Dog.

- を連れた **(o tsureta):** Accompanied by; past form of "連れる" (tsureru).

- 人 **(hito):** People.

- がいます **(ga imasu):** There are (animate objects); polite form.

桜の木が並んでいます。

- **Japanese:** 桜の木が並んでいます。

- **Romaji:** Sakura no ki ga narandeimasu.

- **English:** Cherry blossom trees are lined up.

Grammar and Vocabulary:

- 桜 **(sakura):** Cherry blossoms.

- の **(no):** Possessive particle.

- 木 **(ki):** Tree.

- が **(ga):** Subject marker.

- 並んでいます **(narandeimasu):** Are lined up; polite continuous form of "並ぶ" (narabu).

花はまだ咲いていませんが、蕾があります。

- **Japanese:** 花はまだ咲いていませんが、蕾があります。

- **Romaji:** Hana wa mada saiteimasen ga, tsubomi ga arimasu.

- **English:** The flowers haven't bloomed yet, but there are buds.

Grammar and Vocabulary:

- 花 **(hana):** Flowers.

- は **(wa):** Topic marker.

- まだ **(mada):** Not yet.

- 咲いていません **(saiteimasen):** Haven't bloomed; negative continuous form of "咲く" (saku).

- が **(ga):** But; subject marker.

- 蕾 **(tsubomi):** Buds.

- があります **(ga arimasu):** There are; polite form.

池には鯉が泳いでいます。

- **Japanese:** 池には鯉が泳いでいます。

- **Romaji:** Ike ni wa koi ga oyoideimasu.

- **English:** Koi are swimming in the pond.

Grammar and Vocabulary:

- 池 **(ike):** Pond.

- に **(ni):** Location marker.

- は **(wa):** Topic marker.

- 鯉 **(koi):** Koi (carp).

- が **(ga):** Subject marker.

- 泳いでいます **(oyoideimasu):** Are swimming; polite continuous form of "泳ぐ" (oyogu).

ジョンさんはベンチに座って景色を楽しみます。

- **Japanese:** ジョンさんはベンチに座って景色を楽しみます。

- **Romaji:** Jon-san wa benchi ni suwatte keshiki o tanoshimimasu.

- **English:** John sits on a bench and enjoys the scenery.

Grammar and Vocabulary:

- ジョンさん **(Jon-san):** John.

- は **(wa):** Topic marker.

- ベンチ **(benchi):** Bench.

- に座って **(ni suwatte):** Sits on; te-form of "座る" (suwaru).

- 景色 **(keshiki):** Scenery, view.

- を楽しみます **(o tanoshimimasu):** To enjoy; polite form.

鳥の声が聞こえます。

- **Japanese:** 鳥の声が聞こえます。

- **Romaji:** Tori no koe ga kikoemasu.

- **English:** He can hear the birds' voices.

Grammar and Vocabulary:

- 鳥 **(tori):** Birds.

- の **(no):** Possessive particle.

- 声 **(koe):** Voices.

- が **(ga):** Subject marker.

- 聞こえます **(kikoemasu):** Can hear; polite form of "聞こえる" (kikoeru).

朝の時間は静かで落ち着きます。

- **Japanese:** 朝の時間は静かで落ち着きます。

- **Romaji:** Asa no jikan wa shizuka de ochitsukimasu.

- **English:** The morning time is quiet and calming.

Grammar and Vocabulary:

- 朝の **(asa no):** Morning; "の" indicates possession.

- 時間 **(jikan):** Time.

- は **(wa):** Topic marker.

- 静かで **(shizuka de):** Quiet; "de" connects adjectives.

- 落ち着きます **(ochitsukimasu):** To calm down, to settle; polite form.

一日の良いスタートになりました。

- **Japanese:** 一日の良いスタートになりました。

- **Romaji:** Ichinichi no yoi sutaato ni narimashita.

- **English:** It became a good start to the day.

Grammar and Vocabulary:

- 一日 **(ichinichi):** One day.

- の **(no):** Possessive particle.

- 良い **(yoi):** Good.

- スタート **(sutaato):** Start.

- に **(ni):** Becomes.

- なりました **(narimashita):** Became; past polite form of "なる" (naru).

Story 52: 日本の映画館 (Movie Theater in Japan)

Story in Japanese

ジョンさんは映画館に行きます。

日本のアニメ映画を見ます。

チケットを買って、席に座ります。

ポップコーンを食べながら映画を楽しみます。

日本語の映画ですが、少し理解できます。

ストーリーが面白いです。

映画が終わり、外に出ます。

夜の街は明るいです。

友達と映画の話をします。

楽しい夜でした。

Comprehension Question

ジョンさんは映画館で何を楽しみますか？
(What does John enjoy at the movie theater?)

Story with Line-by-Line Breakdown

ジョンさんは映画館に行きます。

- **Japanese:** ジョンさんは映画館に行きます。

- **Romaji:** Jon-san wa eigakan ni ikimasu.

- **English:** John goes to the movie theater.

Grammar and Vocabulary:

- ジョンさん **(Jon-san):** John.

- は **(wa):** Topic marker.

- 映画館 **(eigakan):** Movie theater.

- に **(ni):** Direction or location marker.

- 行きます **(ikimasu):** To go; polite form.

日本のアニメ映画を見ます。

- **Japanese:** 日本のアニメ映画を見ます。

- **Romaji:** Nihon no anime eiga o mimasu.

- **English:** He watches a Japanese animated movie.

Grammar and Vocabulary:

- 日本の **(Nihon no):** Japanese; "の" indicates possession.

- アニメ映画 **(anime eiga):** Animated movie.

- を見ます **(o mimasu):** To watch; polite form.

チケットを買って、席に座ります。

- **Japanese:** チケットを買って、席に座ります。

- **Romaji:** Chiketto o katte, seki ni suwarimasu.

- **English:** He buys a ticket and sits in his seat.

Grammar and Vocabulary:

- チケット **(chiketto):** Ticket.

- を買って **(o katte):** Buying; te-form of "買う" (kau).

- 席 **(seki):** Seat.

- に座ります **(ni suwarimasu):** To sit in; polite form.

ポップコーンを食べながら映画を楽しみます。

- **Japanese:** ポップコーンを食べながら映画を楽しみます。

- **Romaji:** Poppukōn o tabenagara eiga o tanoshimimasu.

- **English:** He enjoys the movie while eating popcorn.

Grammar and Vocabulary:

- ポップコーン **(poppukōn):** Popcorn.

- を食べながら **(o tabenagara):** While eating; "ながら" indicates simultaneous actions.

- 映画 **(eiga):** Movie.

- を楽しみます **(o tanoshimimasu):** To enjoy; polite form.

日本語の映画ですが、少し理解できます。

- **Japanese:** 日本語の映画ですが、少し理解できます。

- **Romaji:** Nihongo no eiga desu ga, sukoshi rikai dekimasu.

- **English:** It's a Japanese movie, but he can understand a little.

Grammar and Vocabulary:

- 日本語の **(Nihongo no):** Japanese language; "の" indicates possession.

- 映画 **(eiga):** Movie.

- ですが **(desu ga):** But; polite form.

- 少し **(sukoshi):** A little, slightly.

- 理解できます **(rikai dekimasu):** Can understand; polite form.

ストーリーが面白いです。

- **Japanese:** ストーリーが面白いです。

- **Romaji:** Sutōrī ga omoshiroi desu.

- **English:** The story is interesting.

Grammar and Vocabulary:

- ストーリー **(sutōrī):** Story.

- が **(ga):** Subject marker.

- 面白い **(omoshiroi):** Interesting, amusing; "i" adjective.

- です **(desu):** Polite sentence ending.

映画が終わり、外に出ます。

- **Japanese:** 映画が終わり、外に出ます。

- **Romaji:** Eiga ga owari, soto ni demasu.

- **English:** The movie ends, and he goes outside.

Grammar and Vocabulary:

- 映画 **(eiga):** Movie.

- が **(ga):** Subject marker.

- 終わり **(owari):** End.

- 外 **(soto):** Outside.

- に出ます **(ni demasu):** To go out; polite form.

夜の街は明るいです。

- **Japanese:** 夜の街は明るいです。

- **Romaji:** Yoru no machi wa akarui desu.

- **English:** The city at night is bright.

Grammar and Vocabulary:

- 夜の **(yoru no):** Night; "の" indicates possession.

- 街 **(machi):** City, town.

- は **(wa):** Topic marker.

- 明るい **(akarui):** Bright; "i" adjective.

- です **(desu):** Polite sentence ending.

友達と映画の話をします。

- **Japanese:** 友達と映画の話をします。

- **Romaji:** Tomodachi to eiga no hanashi o shimasu.

- **English:** He talks about the movie with his friends.

Grammar and Vocabulary:

- 友達 **(tomodachi):** Friends.

- と **(to):** With.

- 映画の **(eiga no):** Movie's; "の" indicates possession.

- 話 **(hanashi):** Talk, conversation.

- をします **(o shimasu):** To do, to talk about; polite form.

楽しい夜でした。

- **Japanese:** 楽しい夜でした。

- **Romaji:** Tanoshii yoru deshita.

- **English:** It was an enjoyable evening.

Grammar and Vocabulary:

- 楽しい **(tanoshii):** Enjoyable, fun; "i" adjective.

- 夜 **(yoru):** Evening, night.

- でした **(deshita):** Was; past polite form of "です" (desu).

Story 53: 日本のパン屋さん (Japanese Bakery)

Story in Japanese

ジョンさんはパン屋さんに行きます。

美味しそうなパンがたくさんあります。

メロンパンやカレーパンがあります。

ジョンさんはクリームパンを選びます。

店員さんは「ありがとうございます」と言います。

外のベンチでパンを食べます。

とても美味しいです。

日本のパンは種類が多いです。

また来たいと思います。

パン屋さんの匂いが好きです。

Comprehension Question

ジョンさんはパン屋さんで何を選びますか？
(What does John choose at the bakery?)

Story with Line-by-Line Breakdown

ジョンさんはパン屋さんに行きます。

- **Japanese:** ジョンさんはパン屋さんに行きます。

- **Romaji:** Jon-san wa pan'ya-san ni ikimasu.

- **English:** John goes to the bakery.

Grammar and Vocabulary:

- ジョンさん **(Jon-san):** John.

- は **(wa):** Topic marker.

- パン屋さん **(pan'ya-san):** Bakery; "さん" is an honorific suffix.

- に **(ni):** Direction or location marker.

- 行きます **(ikimasu):** To go; polite form.

美味しそうなパンがたくさんあります。

- **Japanese:** 美味しそうなパンがたくさんあります。

- **Romaji:** Oishisou na pan ga takusan arimasu.

- **English:** There are many delicious-looking breads.

Grammar and Vocabulary:

- 美味しそうな **(oishisou na):** Delicious-looking; "そう" indicates appearance, "na" adjective.

- パン **(pan):** Bread.

- が **(ga):** Subject marker.

- たくさん **(takusan):** Many, a lot.

- あります **(arimasu):** There are; polite form.

メロンパンやカレーパンがあります。

- **Japanese:** メロンパンやカレーパンがあります。

- **Romaji:** Meron pan ya karē pan ga arimasu.

- **English:** There are melon breads and curry breads.

Grammar and Vocabulary:

- メロンパン **(meron pan):** Melon bread.

- や **(ya):** And; used to list examples.

- カレーパン **(karē pan):** Curry bread.

- が **(ga):** Subject marker.

- あります **(arimasu):** There are; polite form.

ジョンさんはクリームパンを選びます。

- **Japanese:** ジョンさんはクリームパンを選びます。

- **Romaji:** Jon-san wa kurīmu pan o erabimasu.

- **English:** John chooses a cream bread.

Grammar and Vocabulary:

- ジョンさん **(Jon-san):** John.

- は **(wa):** Topic marker.

- クリームパン **(kurīmu pan):** Cream bread.

- を選びます **(o erabimasu):** To choose; polite form.

店員さんは「ありがとうございます」と言います。

- **Japanese:** 店員さんは「ありがとうございます」と言います。

- **Romaji:** Ten'in-san wa "arigatou gozaimasu" to iimasu.

- **English:** The clerk says, "Thank you."

Grammar and Vocabulary:

- 店員さん **(ten'in-san):** Clerk, store staff; "さん" is an honorific.

- は **(wa):** Topic marker.

- 「ありがとうございます」 **(arigatou gozaimasu):** "Thank you very much."

- と **(to):** Quotation particle.

- 言います **(iimasu):** To say; polite form.

外のベンチでパンを食べます。

- **Japanese:** 外のベンチでパンを食べます。

- **Romaji:** Soto no benchi de pan o tabemasu.

- **English:** He eats bread on an outdoor bench.

Grammar and Vocabulary:

- 外の **(soto no):** Outdoor; "no" indicates possession.

- ベンチ **(benchi):** Bench.

- で **(de):** Location marker indicating where the action takes place.

- パン **(pan):** Bread.

- を食べます **(o tabemasu):** To eat; polite form.

とても美味しいです。

- **Japanese:** とても美味しいです。

- **Romaji:** Totemo oishii desu.

- **English:** It is very delicious.

Grammar and Vocabulary:

- とても **(totemo):** Very.

- 美味しい **(oishii):** Delicious; "i" adjective.

- です **(desu):** Polite sentence ending.

日本のパンは種類が多いです。

- **Japanese:** 日本のパンは種類が多いです。

- **Romaji:** Nihon no pan wa shurui ga ooi desu.

- **English:** Japanese bread comes in many varieties.

Grammar and Vocabulary:

- 日本の **(Nihon no):** Japanese; "の" indicates possession.

- パン **(pan):** Bread.

- は **(wa):** Topic marker.

- 種類 **(shurui):** Variety, type.

- が多い **(ga ooi):** Are many; "多い" (ooi) means "many."

- です **(desu):** Polite sentence ending.

また来たいと思います。

- **Japanese:** また来たいと思います。

- **Romaji:** Mata kitai to omoimasu.

- **English:** He thinks he wants to come again.

Grammar and Vocabulary:

- また **(mata):** Again, also.

- 来たい **(kitai):** Want to come; "たい" form expresses desire.

- と **(to):** Quotation particle.

- 思います **(omoimasu):** To think; polite form.

パン屋さんの匂いが好きです。

- **Japanese:** パン屋さんの匂いが好きです。

- **Romaji:** Pan'ya-san no nioi ga suki desu.

- **English:** He likes the smell of the bakery.

Grammar and Vocabulary:

- パン屋さん **(pan'ya-san):** Bakery; "さん" is an honorific suffix.

- の **(no):** Possessive particle.

- 匂い **(nioi):** Smell, aroma.

- が **(ga):** Subject marker.

- 好きです **(suki desu):** Like; polite form.

Story 54: 日本の花屋さん (Japanese Flower Shop)

How about this bouquet?

Story in Japanese

ジョンさんは花屋さんに入ります。

色とりどりの花があります。

友達へのプレゼントを探します。

店員さんにおすすめを聞きます。

「この花束はいかがですか?」と言われます。

ジョンさんはそれを買います。

友達に花を渡します。

友達はとても喜びます。

花は心を温かくします。

良い買い物ができました。

Comprehension Question

ジョンさんは花屋さんで何を選びますか?
(What does John choose at the flower shop?)

Story with Line-by-Line Breakdown

ジョンさんは花屋さんに入ります。

- **Japanese:** ジョンさんは花屋さんに入ります。

- **Romaji:** Jon-san wa hanaya-san ni hairimasu.
- **English:** John enters the flower shop.

Grammar and Vocabulary:

- ジョンさん **(Jon-san):** John; "さん" is an honorific suffix.
- は **(wa):** Topic marker.
- 花屋さん **(hanaya-san):** Flower shop; "さん" is an honorific suffix.
- に **(ni):** Indicates direction or destination.
- 入ります **(hairimasu):** To enter; polite form.

色とりどりの花があります。

- **Japanese:** 色とりどりの花があります。
- **Romaji:** Irotoridori no hana ga arimasu.
- **English:** There are colorful flowers.

Grammar and Vocabulary:

- 色とりどりの **(irotoridori no):** Colorful; "色とりどり" means "various colors."
- 花 **(hana):** Flower.
- が **(ga):** Subject marker.
- あります **(arimasu):** There are; polite form.

友達へのプレゼントを探します。

- **Japanese:** 友達へのプレゼントを探します。
- **Romaji:** Tomodachi e no purezento o sagashimasu.
- **English:** He looks for a present for his friend.

Grammar and Vocabulary:

- 友達 **(tomodachi):** Friend.

- への **(e no):** For; indicates direction towards someone.

- プレゼント **(purezento):** Present, gift.

- を **(o):** Object marker.

- 探します **(sagashimasu):** To look for; polite form.

店員さんにおすすめを聞きます。

- **Japanese:** 店員さんにおすすめを聞きます。

- **Romaji:** Ten'in-san ni osusume o kikimasu.

- **English:** He asks the clerk for recommendations.

Grammar and Vocabulary:

- 店員さん **(ten'in-san):** Clerk, store staff; "さん" is an honorific.

- に **(ni):** Indicates the person being addressed.

- おすすめ **(osusume):** Recommendation.

- を **(o):** Object marker.

- 聞きます **(kikimasu):** To ask; polite form.

「この花束はいかがですか？」と言われます。

- **Japanese:** 「この花束はいかがですか？」と言われます。

- **Romaji:** "Kono hanataba wa ikaga desu ka?" to iwaremasu.

- **English:** He is asked, "How about this bouquet?"

Grammar and Vocabulary:

- この **(kono):** This.

- 花束 **(hanataba):** Bouquet of flowers.

- は **(wa):** Topic marker.

- いかが **(ikaga):** How about, how is.

- ですか **(desu ka):** Polite question ending.

- と **(to):** Quotation particle.

- 言われます **(iwaremasu):** Is told; passive form of "言う" (iu).

ジョンさんはそれを買います。

- **Japanese:** ジョンさんはそれを買います。

- **Romaji:** Jon-san wa sore o kaimasu.

- **English:** John buys it.

Grammar and Vocabulary:

- ジョンさん **(Jon-san):** John.

- は **(wa):** Topic marker.

- それ **(sore):** That (referring to the bouquet).

- を **(o):** Object marker.

- 買います **(kaimasu):** To buy; polite form.

友達に花を渡します。

- **Japanese:** 友達に花を渡します。

- **Romaji:** Tomodachi ni hana o watashimasu.

- **English:** He gives flowers to his friend.

Grammar and Vocabulary:

- 友達 **(tomodachi):** Friend.

- に **(ni):** Indirect object marker.

- 花 **(hana):** Flowers.

- を渡します **(o watashimasu):** To give; polite form.

友達はとても喜びます。

- **Japanese:** 友達はとても喜びます。

- **Romaji:** Tomodachi wa totemo yorokobimasu.

- **English:** His friend is very happy.

Grammar and Vocabulary:

- 友達 **(tomodachi):** Friend.

- は **(wa):** Topic marker.

- とても **(totemo):** Very.

- 喜びます **(yorokobimasu):** To be happy; polite form.

花は心を温かくします。

- **Japanese:** 花は心を温かくします。

- **Romaji:** Hana wa kokoro o atatakaku shimasu.

- **English:** Flowers warm the heart.

Grammar and Vocabulary:

- 花 **(hana):** Flowers.

- は **(wa):** Topic marker.

- 心 **(kokoro):** Heart, mind.

- を **(o):** Object marker.

- 温かくします **(atatakaku shimasu):** To warm; polite form.

良い買い物ができました。

- **Japanese:** 良い買い物ができました。

- **Romaji:** Yoi kaimono ga dekimashita.

- **English:** He was able to make a good purchase.

Grammar and Vocabulary:

- 良い **(yoi):** Good.

- 買い物 **(kaimono):** Purchase, shopping.

- が **(ga):** Subject marker.

- できました **(dekimashita):** Was able to do; past polite form of "できる" (dekiru).

Story 55: 日本の海辺 (Japanese Seaside)

Story in Japanese

ジョンさんは海に行きます。

砂浜を歩きます。

波の音が心地よいです。

貝殻を拾います。

子供たちが遊んでいます。

ジョンさんはベンチに座って海を眺めます。

風が涼しいです。

海の香りがします。

夕日が沈んでいきます。

美しい景色に感動します。

Comprehension Question

ジョンさんは海辺で何をしますか？
(What does John do at the seaside?)

Story with Line-by-Line Breakdown

ジョンさんは海に行きます。

- **Japanese:** ジョンさんは海に行きます。

- **Romaji:** Jon-san wa umi ni ikimasu.

- **English:** John goes to the sea.

Grammar and Vocabulary:

- ジョンさん **(Jon-san):** John.

- は **(wa):** Topic marker.

- 海 **(umi):** Sea.

- に **(ni):** Direction or location marker.

- 行きます **(ikimasu):** To go; polite form.

砂浜を歩きます。

- **Japanese:** 砂浜を歩きます。

- **Romaji:** Sunahama o arukimasu.

- **English:** He walks on the sandy beach.

Grammar and Vocabulary:

- 砂浜 **(sunahama):** Sandy beach.

- を **(o):** Object marker.

- 歩きます **(arukimasu):** To walk; polite form.

波の音が心地よいです。

- **Japanese:** 波の音が心地よいです。

- **Romaji:** Nami no oto ga kokochi yoi desu.

- **English:** The sound of the waves is pleasant.

Grammar and Vocabulary:

- 波 **(nami):** Waves.

- の **(no):** Possessive particle.

- 音 **(oto):** Sound.

- が **(ga):** Subject marker.

- 心地よい **(kokochi yoi):** Pleasant, comfortable; "i" adjective.

- です **(desu):** Polite sentence ending.

貝殻を拾います。

- **Japanese:** 貝殻を拾います。

- **Romaji:** Kaigara o hiroumasu.

- **English:** He picks up seashells.

Grammar and Vocabulary:

- 貝殻 **(kaigara):** Seashells.

- を **(o):** Object marker.

- 拾います **(hiroumasu):** To pick up; polite form.

子供たちが遊んでいます。

- **Japanese:** 子供たちが遊んでいます。

- **Romaji:** Kodomotachi ga asondeimasu.

- **English:** Children are playing.

Grammar and Vocabulary:

- 子供たち **(kodomotachi):** Children.

- が **(ga):** Subject marker.

- 遊んでいます **(asondeimasu):** Are playing; polite continuous form of "遊ぶ" (asobu).

ジョンさんはベンチに座って海を眺めます。

- **Japanese:** ジョンさんはベンチに座って海を眺めます。

- **Romaji:** Jon-san wa benchi ni suwatte umi o nagamemasu.

- **English:** John sits on a bench and gazes at the sea.

Grammar and Vocabulary:

- ジョンさん **(Jon-san):** John.

- は **(wa):** Topic marker.

- ベンチ **(benchi):** Bench.

- に座って **(ni suwatte):** Sits on; te-form of "座る" (suwaru).

- 海 **(umi):** Sea.

- を眺めます **(o nagamemasu):** To gaze at; polite form.

風が涼しいです。

- **Japanese:** 風が涼しいです。

- **Romaji:** Kaze ga suzushii desu.

- **English:** The breeze is cool.

Grammar and Vocabulary:

- 風 **(kaze):** Breeze, wind.

- が **(ga):** Subject marker.

- 涼しい **(suzushii):** Cool; "i" adjective.

- です **(desu):** Polite sentence ending.

海の香りがします。

- **Japanese:** 海の香りがします。

- **Romaji:** Umi no kaori ga shimasu.

- **English:** He smells the scent of the sea.

Grammar and Vocabulary:

- 海 **(umi):** Sea.

- の **(no):** Possessive particle.

- 香り **(kaori):** Scent, aroma.

- が **(ga):** Subject marker.

- します **(shimasu):** To smell; polite form.

夕日が沈んでいきます。

- **Japanese:** 夕日が沈んでいきます。

- **Romaji:** Yuuhi ga shizunde ikimasu.

- **English:** The sunset sinks.

Grammar and Vocabulary:

- 夕日 **(yuuhi):** Sunset.

- が **(ga):** Subject marker.

- 沈んでいきます **(shizunde ikimasu):** Sinks; polite form of "沈む" (shizumu) + "いく" (iku) indicating continuation.

美しい景色に感動します。

- **Japanese:** 美しい景色に感動します。

- **Romaji:** Utsukushii keshiki ni kandou shimasu.

- **English:** He is moved by the beautiful scenery.

Grammar and Vocabulary:

- 美しい **(utsukushii):** Beautiful; "i" adjective.

- 景色 **(keshiki):** Scenery, view.

- に **(ni):** Indicates the cause or reason.

- 感動します **(kandou shimasu):** To be moved, touched; polite form.

Story 56: 日本の博物館 (Japanese Museum)

Story in Japanese

ジョンさんは博物館に行きます。

日本の歴史を学びます。

昔の道具や衣服があります。

説明を読みながら見学します。

刀や鎧が展示されています。

とても興味深いです。

時間をかけてゆっくり見ます。

日本の文化に触れることができます。

博物館を出て、知識が増えたと感じます。

有意義な一日でした。

Comprehension Question

ジョンさんは博物館で何を学びますか？
(What does John learn at the museum?)

Story with Line-by-Line Breakdown

ジョンさんは博物館に行きます。

- **Japanese:** ジョンさんは博物館に行きます。

- **Romaji:** Jon-san wa hakubutsukan ni ikimasu.

- **English:** John goes to the museum.

Grammar and Vocabulary:

- ジョンさん **(Jon-san):** John.

- は **(wa):** Topic marker.

- 博物館 **(hakubutsukan):** Museum.

- に **(ni):** Direction or location marker.

- 行きます **(ikimasu):** To go; polite form.

日本の歴史を学びます。

- **Japanese:** 日本の歴史を学びます。

- **Romaji:** Nihon no rekishi o manabimasu.

- **English:** He studies Japanese history.

Grammar and Vocabulary:

- 日本の **(Nihon no):** Japanese; "の" indicates possession.

- 歴史 **(rekishi):** History.

- を **(o):** Object marker.

- 学びます **(manabimasu):** To study, to learn; polite form.

昔の道具や衣服があります。

- **Japanese:** 昔の道具や衣服があります。

- **Romaji:** Mukashi no dougu ya ifuku ga arimasu.

- **English:** There are old tools and clothes.

Grammar and Vocabulary:

- 昔の **(mukashi no):** Old; "の" indicates possession.

- 道具 **(dougu):** Tools, utensils.

- や **(ya):** And; used to list examples.

- 衣服 **(ifuku):** Clothes.

- が **(ga):** Subject marker.

- あります **(arimasu):** There are; polite form.

説明を読みながら見学します。

- **Japanese:** 説明を読みながら見学します。

- **Romaji:** Setsumei o yominagara kengaku shimasu.

- **English:** He tours the museum while reading explanations.

Grammar and Vocabulary:

- 説明 **(setsumei):** Explanation.

- を **(o):** Object marker.

- 読みながら **(yominagara):** While reading; "ながら" indicates simultaneous actions.

- 見学します **(kengaku shimasu):** To tour, to observe; polite form.

刀や鎧が展示されています。

- **Japanese:** 刀や鎧が展示されています。

- **Romaji:** Katana ya yoroi ga tenji sareteimasu.

- **English:** Swords and armor are on display.

Grammar and Vocabulary:

- 刀 **(katana):** Sword.

- や **(ya):** And; used to list examples.

- 鎧 **(yoroi):** Armor.

- が **(ga):** Subject marker.

- 展示されています **(tenji sareteimasu):** Are on display; passive continuous form of "展示する" (tenji suru).

とても興味深いです。

- **Japanese:** とても興味深いです。

- **Romaji:** Totemo kyoumi-bukai desu.

- **English:** It is very interesting.

Grammar and Vocabulary:

- とても **(totemo):** Very.

- 興味深い **(kyoumi-bukai):** Interesting, fascinating; "i" adjective.

- です **(desu):** Polite sentence ending.

時間をかけてゆっくり見ます。

- **Japanese:** 時間をかけてゆっくり見ます。

- **Romaji:** Jikan o kakete yukkuri mimasu.

- **English:** He takes his time to look around.

Grammar and Vocabulary:

- 時間 **(jikan):** Time.

- をかけて **(o kakete):** Taking time; "かける" means "to spend (time)."

- ゆっくり **(yukkuri):** Slowly, leisurely.

- 見ます **(mimasu):** To look, to see; polite form.

日本の文化に触れることができます。

- **Japanese:** 日本の文化に触れることができます。

- **Romaji:** Nihon no bunka ni fureru koto ga dekimasu.

- **English:** He can experience Japanese culture.

Grammar and Vocabulary:

- 日本の **(Nihon no):** Japanese; "の" indicates possession.

- 文化 **(bunka):** Culture.

- に触れる **(ni fureru)**: To touch upon, to experience.

- ことができます **(koto ga dekimasu)**: Can do; polite form.

博物館を出て、知識が増えたと感じます。

- **Japanese:** 博物館を出て、知識が増えたと感じます。

- **Romaji:** Hakubutsukan o dete, chishiki ga fueta to kanjimasu.

- **English:** He leaves the museum feeling that his knowledge has increased.

Grammar and Vocabulary:

- 博物館 **(hakubutsukan)**: Museum.

- を出て **(o dete)**: Leaving; te-form of "出る" (deru).

- 知識 **(chishiki)**: Knowledge.

- が増えた **(ga fueta)**: Has increased; past form of "増える" (fueru).

- と感じます **(to kanjimasu)**: Feels that; polite form.

有意義な一日でした。

- **Japanese:** 有意義な一日でした。

- **Romaji:** Yūigi na ichinichi deshita.

- **English:** It was a meaningful day.

Grammar and Vocabulary:

- 有意義な **(yūigi na)**: Meaningful; "na" adjective.

- 一日 **(ichinichi)**: One day.

- でした **(deshita)**: Was; past polite form of "です" (desu).

Story 57: 日本の夜の散歩 (Night Walk in Japan)

Story in Japanese

夜、ジョンさんは街を散歩します。

ネオンの光が輝いています。

人々が行き交っています。

屋台から美味しそうな匂いがします。

たこ焼きを買って食べます。

熱くて美味しいです。

音楽が聞こえてきます。

小さなライブハウスがあります。

少し立ち寄って音楽を聴きます。

夜の街も魅力的です。

Comprehension Question

ジョンさんは夜の散歩で何をしますか？
(What does John do during his night walk?)

Story with Line-by-Line Breakdown

夜、ジョンさんは街を散歩します。

- **Japanese:** 夜、ジョンさんは街を散歩します。

- **Romaji:** Yoru, Jon-san wa machi o sanpo shimasu.

- **English:** At night, John takes a walk through the city.

Grammar and Vocabulary:

- 夜 **(yoru):** Night.

- 、(、): Comma, indicating a pause.

- ジョンさん (Jon-san): John.

- は (wa): Topic marker.

- 街 (machi): City, town.

- を散歩します (o sanpo shimasu): To take a walk; polite form.

ネオンの光が輝いています。

- **Japanese:** ネオンの光が輝いています。

- **Romaji:** Neon no hikari ga kagayaiteimasu.

- **English:** Neon lights are shining.

Grammar and Vocabulary:

- ネオン (neon): Neon.

- の (no): Possessive particle.

- 光 (hikari): Light.

- が (ga): Subject marker.

- 輝いています (kagayaiteimasu): Are shining; polite continuous form of "輝く" (kagayaku).

人々が行き交っています。

- **Japanese:** 人々が行き交っています。

- **Romaji:** Hitobito ga ikikatteimasu.

- **English:** People are coming and going.

Grammar and Vocabulary:

- 人々 (hitobito): People.

- が (ga): Subject marker.

- 行き交っています **(ikikatteimasu):** Are coming and going; polite continuous form of "行き交う" (ikikau).

屋台から美味しそうな匂いがします。

- **Japanese:** 屋台から美味しそうな匂いがします。

- **Romaji:** Yatai kara oishisou na nioi ga shimasu.

- **English:** Delicious-looking smells come from the food stalls.

Grammar and Vocabulary:

- 屋台 **(yatai):** Food stall, street vendor.

- から **(kara):** From.

- 美味しそうな **(oishisou na):** Delicious-looking; "そう" indicates appearance, "な" adjective.

- 匂い **(nioi):** Smell, aroma.

- が **(ga):** Subject marker.

- します **(shimasu):** To smell; polite form.

たこ焼きを買って食べます。

- **Japanese:** たこ焼きを買って食べます。

- **Romaji:** Takoyaki o katte tabemasu.

- **English:** He buys and eats takoyaki.

Grammar and Vocabulary:

- たこ焼き **(takoyaki):** Takoyaki (octopus-filled batter balls).

- を買って **(o katte):** Buying; te-form of "買う" (kau).

- 食べます **(tabemasu):** To eat; polite form.

熱くて美味しいです。

- **Japanese:** 熱くて美味しいです。

- **Romaji:** Atsukute oishii desu.

- **English:** They are hot and delicious.

Grammar and Vocabulary:

- 熱くて **(atsukute):** Hot; te-form of "熱い" (atsui).

- 美味しい **(oishii):** Delicious; "i" adjective.

- です **(desu):** Polite sentence ending.

音楽が聞こえてきます。

- **Japanese:** 音楽が聞こえてきます。

- **Romaji:** Ongaku ga kikoete kimasu.

- **English:** Music starts to be heard.

Grammar and Vocabulary:

- 音楽 **(ongaku):** Music.

- が **(ga):** Subject marker.

- 聞こえてきます **(kikoete kimasu):** Starts to be heard; combination of "聞こえる" (kikoeru) and "くる" (kuru).

小さなライブハウスがあります。

- **Japanese:** 小さなライブハウスがあります。

- **Romaji:** Chiisana raibu hausu ga arimasu.

- **English:** There is a small live house.

Grammar and Vocabulary:

- 小さな **(chiisana):** Small; "na" adjective.

- ライブハウス **(raibu hausu):** Live house (small live music venue).

- が **(ga):** Subject marker.

- あります **(arimasu):** There are; polite form.

少し立ち寄って音楽を聴きます。

- **Japanese:** 少し立ち寄って音楽を聴きます。

- **Romaji:** Sukoshi tachiyoratte ongaku o kikimasu.

- **English:** He stops by briefly and listens to music.

Grammar and Vocabulary:

- 少し **(sukoshi):** A little, briefly.

- 立ち寄って **(tachiyoratte):** Stopping by; te-form of "立ち寄る" (tachiyoru).

- 音楽 **(ongaku):** Music.

- を聴きます **(o kikimasu):** To listen to; polite form.

夜の街も魅力的です。

- **Japanese:** 夜の街も魅力的です。

- **Romaji:** Yoru no machi mo miryokuteki desu.

- **English:** The city at night is also charming.

Grammar and Vocabulary:

- 夜の **(yoru no):** Night; "の" indicates possession.

- 街 **(machi):** City, town.

- も **(mo):** Also, too.

- 魅力的 **(miryokuteki):** Charming, attractive; "na" adjective.

- です **(desu):** Polite sentence ending.

Story 58: 日本の山村 (Japanese Mountain Village)

Story in Japanese

ジョンさんは山の村に行きます。

自然がいっぱいです。

古い木造の家があります。

村の人々は親切です。

小さな川が流れています。

鳥の声が聞こえます。

ジョンさんは散歩をします。

静かな時間を過ごします。

空気が美味しいです。

心が癒されます。

Comprehension Question

ジョンさんは山村で何を感じますか？
(What does John feel in the mountain village?)

Story with Line-by-Line Breakdown

ジョンさんは山の村に行きます。

- **Japanese:** ジョンさんは山の村に行きます。

- **Romaji:** Jon-san wa yama no mura ni ikimasu.

- **English:** John goes to a mountain village.

Grammar and Vocabulary:

- ジョンさん **(Jon-san):** John.

- は **(wa):** Topic marker.

- 山の村 **(yama no mura):** Mountain village; "の" indicates possession.

- に **(ni):** Direction or location marker.

- 行きます **(ikimasu):** To go; polite form.

自然がいっぱいです。

- **Japanese:** 自然がいっぱいです。

- **Romaji:** Shizen ga ippai desu.

- **English:** Nature is abundant.

- **Grammar and Vocabulary:**

- 自然 **(shizen):** Nature.

- が **(ga):** Subject marker.

- いっぱい **(ippai):** Full, abundant.

- です **(desu):** Polite sentence ending.

古い木造の家があります。

- **Japanese:** 古い木造の家があります。

- **Romaji:** Furui mokuzou no ie ga arimasu.

- **English:** There are old wooden houses.

Grammar and Vocabulary:

- 古い **(furui):** Old; "i" adjective.

- 木造の **(mokuzou no):** Wooden; "木造" means "wooden construction."

- 家 **(ie):** House.

- が **(ga):** Subject marker.

- あります **(arimasu):** There are; polite form.

村の人々は親切です。

- **Japanese:** 村の人々は親切です。

- **Romaji:** Mura no hitobito wa shinsetsu desu.

- **English:** The villagers are kind.

Grammar and Vocabulary:

- 村の **(mura no):** Village's; "の" indicates possession.

- 人々 **(hitobito):** People, villagers.

- は **(wa):** Topic marker.

- 親切 **(shinsetsu):** Kindness; "na" adjective.

- です **(desu):** Polite sentence ending.

小さな川が流れています。

- **Japanese:** 小さな川が流れています。

- **Romaji:** Chiisana kawa ga nagareteimasu.

- **English:** A small river is flowing.

Grammar and Vocabulary:

- 小さな **(chiisana):** Small; "na" adjective.

- 川 **(kawa):** River.

- が **(ga):** Subject marker.

- 流れています **(nagareteimasu):** Is flowing; polite continuous form of "流れる" (nagareru).

鳥の声が聞こえます。

- **Japanese:** 鳥の声が聞こえます。

- **Romaji:** Tori no koe ga kikoemasu.

- **English:** He can hear the birds' songs.

Grammar and Vocabulary:

- 鳥 **(tori):** Birds.

- の **(no):** Possessive particle.

- 声 **(koe):** Voice, song.

- が **(ga):** Subject marker.

- 聞こえます **(kikoemasu):** Can hear; polite form of "聞こえる" (kikoeru).

ジョンさんは散歩をします。

- **Japanese:** ジョンさんは散歩をします。

- **Romaji:** Jon-san wa sanpo o shimasu.

- **English:** John takes a walk.

Grammar and Vocabulary:

- ジョンさん **(Jon-san):** John.

- は **(wa):** Topic marker.

- 散歩 **(sanpo):** Walk, stroll.

- をします **(o shimasu):** To do; polite form.

静かな時間を過ごします。

- **Japanese:** 静かな時間を過ごします。

- **Romaji:** Shizuka na jikan o sugoshimasu.

- **English:** He spends quiet time.

Grammar and Vocabulary:

- 静かな **(shizuka na):** Quiet; "na" adjective.

- 時間 **(jikan):** Time.

- を過ごします **(o sugoshimasu):** To spend; polite form.

空気が美味しいです。

- **Japanese:** 空気が美味しいです。

- **Romaji:** Kuuki ga oishii desu.

- **English:** The air is delicious (fresh).

Grammar and Vocabulary:

- 空気 **(kuuki):** Air.

- が **(ga):** Subject marker.

- 美味しい **(oishii):** Delicious; often used metaphorically for "fresh" when referring to air.

- です **(desu):** Polite sentence ending.

心が癒されます。

- **Japanese:** 心が癒されます。

- **Romaji:** Kokoro ga iyasaremasu.

- **English:** His heart is healed, he feels soothed.

Grammar and Vocabulary:

- 心 **(kokoro):** Heart, mind.

- が **(ga):** Subject marker.

- 癒されます **(iyasaremasu):** Is healed, is soothed; passive form of "癒す" (iyasu).

Story 59: 日本の陶芸体験 (Japanese Pottery Experience)

Story in Japanese

ジョンさんは陶芸教室に参加します。

粘土を使ってお皿を作ります。

先生が作り方を教えてくれます。

形を整えるのが難しいです。

でも楽しいです。

自分だけの作品ができます。

焼き上がりが楽しみです。

陶芸は集中できる良い時間です。

新しい趣味が見つかりました。

また挑戦したいです。

Comprehension Question

ジョンさんは陶芸教室で何を作りますか？
(What does John make in the pottery class?)

Story with Line-by-Line Breakdown

ジョンさんは陶芸教室に参加します。

- **Japanese:** ジョンさんは陶芸教室に参加します。

- **Romaji:** Jon-san wa toujoukyoushitsu ni sanka shimasu.

- **English:** John participates in a pottery class.

Grammar and Vocabulary:

- ジョンさん (Jon-san): John (with honorific "san").

- は (wa): Topic marker.

- 陶芸教室 (tougei kyoushitsu): Pottery class.

- に (ni): Indicates destination or target.

- 参加します (sanka shimasu): To participate; polite form.

粘土を使ってお皿を作ります。

- **Japanese:** 粘土を使ってお皿を作ります。

- **Romaji:** Nendo o tsukatte osara o tsukurimasu.

- **English:** He makes a plate using clay.

Grammar and Vocabulary:

- 粘土 (nendo): Clay.

- を (o): Object marker.

- 使って (tsukatte): Using; te-form of "使う" (to use).

- お皿 (osara): Plate.

- 作ります (tsukurimasu): To make; polite form.

先生が作り方を教えてくれます。

- **Japanese:** 先生が作り方を教えてくれます。

- **Romaji:** Sensei ga tsukurikata o oshiete kuremasu.

- **English:** The teacher teaches him how to make it.

Grammar and Vocabulary:

- 先生 (sensei): Teacher.

- が (ga): Subject marker.

- 作り方 (tsukurikata): How to make; method.

- を (o): Object marker.

- 教えてくれます (oshiete kuremasu): Teaches (with the nuance of doing a favor); polite form.

形を整えるのが難しいです。

- **Japanese:** 形を整えるのが難しいです。

- **Romaji:** Katachi o totonoeru no ga muzukashii desu.

- **English:** Shaping it is difficult.

Grammar and Vocabulary:

- 形 (katachi): Shape.

- を (o): Object marker.

- 整える (totonoeru): To shape, to arrange.

- のが (no ga): Nominalizer + subject marker.

- 難しい (muzukashii): Difficult; "i" adjective.

- です (desu): Polite sentence ending.

でも楽しいです。

- **Japanese:** でも楽しいです。

- **Romaji:** Demo tanoshii desu.

- **English:** But it's fun.

Grammar and Vocabulary:

- でも (demo): But.

- 楽しい (tanoshii): Fun; "i" adjective.

- です (desu): Polite sentence ending.

自分だけの作品ができます。

- **Japanese:** 自分だけの作品ができます。

- **Romaji:** Jibun dake no sakuhin ga dekimasu.

- **English:** He can create his own unique work.

Grammar and Vocabulary:

- 自分だけの (jibun dake no): One's own; unique.

- 作品 (sakuhin): Work (of art).

- が (ga): Subject marker.

- できます (dekimasu): Can do; polite form.

焼き上がりが楽しみです。

- **Japanese:** 焼き上がりが楽しみです。

- **Romaji:** Yakiagari ga tanoshimi desu.

- **English:** He is looking forward to the firing completion.

Grammar and Vocabulary:

- 焼き上がり (yakiagari): Completion of firing (in pottery).

- が (ga): Subject marker.

- 楽しみ (tanoshimi): Looking forward to; noun form.

- です (desu): Polite sentence ending.

陶芸は集中できる良い時間です。

- **Japanese:** 陶芸は集中できる良い時間です。

- **Romaji:** Tougei wa shuuchuu dekiru yoi jikan desu.

- **English:** Pottery is a good time to concentrate.

Grammar and Vocabulary:

- 陶芸 (tougei): Pottery.

- は (wa): Topic marker.

- 集中できる (shuuchuu dekiru): Can concentrate; potential form.

- 良い (yoi): Good; "i" adjective.

- 時間 (jikan): Time.

- です (desu): Polite sentence ending.

新しい趣味が見つかりました。

- **Japanese:** 新しい趣味が見つかりました。

- **Romaji:** Atarashii shumi ga mitsukarimashita.

- **English:** He found a new hobby.

Grammar and Vocabulary:

- 新しい (atarashii): New; "i" adjective.

- 趣味 (shumi): Hobby.

- が (ga): Subject marker.

- 見つかりました (mitsukarimashita): Found; past polite form.

また挑戦したいです。

- **Japanese:** また挑戦したいです。

- **Romaji:** Mata chousen shitai desu.

- **English:** He wants to challenge himself again.

Grammar and Vocabulary:

- また (mata): Again.

- 挑戦したい (chousen shitai): Want to challenge; "tai" form expresses desire.

- です (desu): Polite sentence ending.

Story 60: 日本の別れ (Farewell in Japan)

Story in Japanese

ジョンさんの旅は終わりに近づきます。

日本での時間を思い出します。

たくさんの人に出会いました。

美しい場所を訪れました。

日本語も少し上達しました。

友達にお礼を言います。

「また会いましょう」と約束します。

荷物をまとめて空港に向かいます。

飛行機に乗る前に、日本の風景をもう一度見ます。

「ありがとう、日本」と心の中でつぶやきます。

Comprehension Question

ジョンさんは日本でどんな経験をしましたか？
(What kind of experiences did John have in Japan?)

Story with Line-by-Line Breakdown

ジョンさんの旅は終わりに近づきます。

- **Japanese:** ジョンさんの旅は終わりに近づきます。

- **Romaji:** Jon-san no tabi wa owari ni chikazukimasu.

- **English:** John's journey is approaching its end.

Grammar and Vocabulary:

- ジョンさん (Jon-san): John (with honorific "san").

- の (no): Possessive particle ("'s").

- 旅 (tabi): Journey, trip.

- は (wa): Topic marker.

- 終わり (owari): End.

- に (ni): Indicates direction or target.

- 近づきます (chikazukimasu): To approach; polite form.

日本での時間を思い出します。

- **Japanese:** 日本での時間を思い出します。

- **Romaji:** Nihon de no jikan o omoidasu masu.

- **English:** He recalls his time in Japan.

Grammar and Vocabulary:

- 日本 (Nihon): Japan.

- で (de): Indicates location of action.

- の (no): Possessive particle ("of").

- 時間 (jikan): Time.

- を (o): Object marker.

- 思い出します (omoidasu masu): To recall, remember; polite form.

たくさんの人に出会いました。

- **Japanese:** たくさんの人に出会いました。

- **Romaji:** Takusan no hito ni deaimashita.

- **English:** He met many people.

Grammar and Vocabulary:

- たくさんの (takusan no): Many, a lot of.

- 人 (hito): People.

- に (ni): Indicates the target of the action.

- 出会いました (deaimashita): Met; past polite form.

美しい場所を訪れました。

- **Japanese:** 美しい場所を訪れました。

- **Romaji:** Utsukushii basho o otozuremashita.

- **English:** He visited beautiful places.

Grammar and Vocabulary:

- 美しい (utsukushii): Beautiful; "i" adjective.

- 場所 (basho): Place.

- を (o): Object marker.

- 訪れました (otozuremashita): Visited; past polite form.

日本語も少し上達しました。

- **Japanese:** 日本語も少し上達しました。

- **Romaji:** Nihongo mo sukoshi joutatsu shimashita.

- **English:** His Japanese also improved a little.

Grammar and Vocabulary:

- 日本語 (nihongo): Japanese language.

- も (mo): Also, too.

- 少し (sukoshi): A little.

- 上達しました (joutatsu shimashita): Improved; past polite form.

友達にお礼を言います。

- **Japanese:** 友達にお礼を言います。

- **Romaji:** Tomodachi ni orei o iimasu.

- **English:** He thanks his friends.

Grammar and Vocabulary:

- 友達 (tomodachi): Friends.

- に (ni): Indicates the target of the action.

- お礼 (orei): Thanks, gratitude.

- を (o): Object marker.

- 言います (iimasu): To say; polite form.

「また会いましょう」と約束します。

- **Japanese:** 「また会いましょう」と約束します。

- **Romaji:** "Mata aimashou" to yakusoku shimasu.

- **English:** He promises, "Let's meet again."

Grammar and Vocabulary:

- また (mata): Again.

- 会いましょう (aimashou): Let's meet; volitional form.

- と (to): Quotation particle.

- 約束します (yakusoku shimasu): To promise; polite form.

荷物をまとめて空港に向かいます。

- **Japanese:** 荷物をまとめて空港に向かいます。

- **Romaji:** Nimotsu o matomete kuukou ni mukaimasu.

- **English:** He packs his luggage and heads to the airport.

Grammar and Vocabulary:

- 荷物 (nimotsu): Luggage, baggage.

- を (o): Object marker.

- まとめて (matomete): Packing, putting together; te-form of "まとめる" (to pack).

- 空港 (kuukou): Airport.

- に (ni): Indicates direction.

- 向かいます (mukaimasu): To head towards; polite form.

飛行機に乗る前に、日本の風景をもう一度見ます。

- **Japanese:** 飛行機に乗る前に、日本の風景をもう一度見ます。

- **Romaji:** Hikouki ni noru mae ni, Nihon no fuukei o mou ichido mimasu.

- **English:** Before boarding the plane, he looks at the Japanese scenery once more.

Grammar and Vocabulary:

- 飛行機 (hikouki): Airplane.

- に (ni): Indicates target of action.

- 乗る (noru): To board, to get on.

- 前に (mae ni): Before.

- 日本 (Nihon): Japan.

- の (no): Possessive particle ("of").

- 風景 (fuukei): Scenery.

- を (o): Object marker.

- もう一度 (mou ichido): Once more.

- 見ます (mimasu): To see; polite form.

「ありがとう、日本」と心の中でつぶやきます。

- **Japanese:** 「ありがとう、日本」と心の中でつぶやきます。

- **Romaji:** "Arigatou, Nihon" to kokoro no naka de tsubuyakimasu.

- **English:** He whispers to himself, "Thank you, Japan."

Grammar and Vocabulary:

- ありがとう (arigatou): Thank you.

- 日本 (Nihon): Japan.

- と (to): Quotation particle.

- 心の中で (kokoro no naka de): In his heart, to himself.

- つぶやきます (tsubuyakimasu): To whisper; polite form.

Essential Kanji

Kanji	Furigana	Romaji	English Translation
一	いち	ichi	one
二	に	ni	two
三	さん	san	three
四	し / よん	shi / yon	four
五	ご	go	five
六	ろく	roku	six
七	しち / なな	shichi / nana	seven
八	はち	hachi	eight
九	きゅう / く	kyū / ku	nine
十	じゅう	jū	ten
百	ひゃく	hyaku	hundred
千	せん	sen	thousand
万	まん	man	ten thousand
日	ひ / にち	hi / nichi	day, sun
月	つき / げつ	tsuki / getsu	moon, month
火	ひ / か	hi / ka	fire
水	みず / すい	mizu / sui	water

木	き / もく	ki / moku	tree, wood
金	かね / きん	kane / kin	gold, money
土	つち / ど	tsuchi / do	earth, soil
山	やま	yama	mountain
川	かわ	kawa	river
田	た / でん	ta / den	rice field
人	ひと / じん / にん	hito / jin / nin	person
口	くち	kuchi	mouth
目	め	me	eye
耳	みみ	mimi	ear
手	て	te	hand
足	あし	ashi	foot, leg
上	うえ / じょう	ue / jō	up, above
下	した / か	shita / ka	down, below
中	なか / ちゅう	naka / chū	inside, middle
左	ひだり	hidari	left
右	みぎ	migi	right
大	おお / だい	ō / dai	big
小	ちい / しょう	chii / shō	small
高	たか / こう	taka / kō	high, expensive
安	やす / あん	yasu / an	cheap, safe
新	あたら / しん	atara / shin	new
古	ふる / こ	furu / ko	old
学	まな / がく	mana / gaku	study, learning
校	こう	kō	school
先	さき / せん	saki / sen	previous, ahead
生	い / せい	i / sei	life, birth
何	なに / なん	nani / nan	what
年	とし / ねん	toshi / nen	year
時	とき / じ	toki / ji	time, hour
分	わ / ふん	wa / fun	minute, divide
半	なか / はん	naka / han	half

友	とも	tomo	friend
父	ちち / ふ	chichi / fu	father
母	はは / ぼ	haha / bo	mother
男	おとこ / だん	otoko / dan	man
女	おんな / じょ	onna / jo	woman
子	こ / し	ko / shi	child
天	てん	ten	heaven, sky
気	き	ki	spirit, mind
見	み / けん	mi / ken	see, look
行	い / こう	i / kō	go
来	く / らい	ku / rai	come
食	た / しょく	ta / shoku	eat
飲	の / いん	no / in	drink
会	あ / かい	a / kai	meet, meeting
話	はな / わ	hana / wa	speak, talk
読	よ / どく	yo / doku	read
書	か / しょ	ka / sho	write
買	か / ばい	ka / bai	buy
入	はい / にゅう	hai / nyū	enter
出	で / しゅつ	de / shutsu	exit
休	やす / きゅう	yasu / kyū	rest
名	な / めい	na / mei	name
白	しろ / はく	shiro / haku	white
天気	てんき	tenki	weather
電	でん	den	electricity
車	くるま / しゃ	kuruma / sha	car
駅	えき	eki	station
社	やしろ / しゃ	yashiro / sha	company, shrine
国	くに / こく	kuni / koku	country
毎	まい	mai	every
話	はなし / わ	hanashi / wa	story, talk
言	い / げん	i / gen	say, word

語	かた / ご	kata / go	language, word
聞	き / ぶん	ki / bun	hear, listen
東	ひがし / とう	higashi / tō	east
西	にし / せい	nishi / sei	west
南	みなみ / なん	minami / nan	south
北	きた / ほく	kita / hoku	north
午	ご	go	noon
後	あと / ご	ato / go	after, behind
前	まえ / ぜん	mae / zen	before, front
間	あいだ / かん	aida / kan	between, interval
道	みち / どう	michi / dō	road, way
電話	でんわ	denwa	telephone
先生	せんせい	sensei	teacher
学生	がくせい	gakusei	student
来年	らいねん	rainen	next year
去年	きょねん	kyonen	last year
今日	きょう	kyō	today
明日	あした	ashita	tomorrow
昨日	きのう	kinō	yesterday
今	いま	ima	now
午前	ごぜん	gozen	morning, a.m.
午後	ごご	gogo	afternoon, p.m.

Note: Some kanji have multiple readings and meanings depending on the context.
The readings

Essential Vocabulary – Kanji Optional

Kanji	Furigana	Romaji	English Translation
青	あお	ao	blue
赤	あか	aka	red
明るい	あかるい	akarui	bright
秋	あき	aki	autumn
開ける	あける	akeru	to open
朝	あさ	asa	morning

朝ご飯	あさごはん	asagohan	breakfast
遊ぶ	あそぶ	asobu	to play
暖かい	あたたかい	atatakai	warm
頭	あたま	atama	head
新しい	あたらしい	atarashii	new
暑い	あつい	atsui	hot (weather)
熱い	あつい	atsui	hot (objects)
厚い	あつい	atsui	thick
後	あと	ato	later, after
兄	あに	ani	older brother
姉	あね	ane	older sister
余り	あまり	amari	not very (with neg.)
雨	あめ	ame	rain
飴	あめ	ame	candy
洗う	あらう	arau	to wash
歩く	あるく	aruku	to walk
ある	ある	aru	to exist (inanimate)
安い	やすい	yasui	cheap
家	いえ	ie	house
行く	いく	iku	to go
池	いけ	ike	pond
医者	いしゃ	isha	doctor
忙しい	いそがしい	isogashii	busy
痛い	いたい	itai	painful
一緒	いっしょ	issho	together
五つ	いつつ	itsutsu	five things
犬	いぬ	inu	dog
今朝	けさ	kesa	this morning
意味	いみ	imi	meaning
妹	いもうと	imōto	younger sister
嫌い	きらい	kirai	dislike
入口	いりぐち	iriguchi	entrance

要る	いる	iru	to need
入れる	いれる	ireru	to put in
色	いろ	iro	color
色々	いろいろ	iroiro	various
後ろ	うしろ	ushiro	behind
薄い	うすい	usui	thin
歌	うた	uta	song
歌う	うたう	utau	to sing
生まれる	うまれる	umareru	to be born
海	うみ	umi	sea
売る	うる	uru	to sell
上着	うわぎ	uwagi	jacket
映画	えいが	eiga	movie
映画館	えいがかん	eigakan	cinema
英語	えいご	eigo	English language
駅	えき	eki	station
エレベーター		erebētā	elevator
円	えん	en	yen
鉛筆	えんぴつ	enpitsu	pencil
美味しい	おいしい	oishii	delicious
多い	おおい	ooi	many
大きい	おおきい	ōkii	big
お母さん	おかあさん	okāsan	mother
お菓子	おかし	okashi	sweets
お金	おかね	okane	money
起きる	おきる	okiru	to get up
奥さん	おくさん	okusan	wife
お酒	おさけ	osake	alcohol
お皿	おさら	osara	plate
教える	おしえる	oshieru	to teach
押す	おす	osu	to push

遅い	おそい	osoi	late
お茶	おちゃ	ocha	tea
お手洗い	おてあらい	otearai	restroom
お父さん	おとうさん	otōsan	father
弟	おとうと	otōto	younger brother
男の子	おとこのこ	otokonoko	boy
一昨日	おととい	ototoi	day before yesterday
一昨年	おととし	ototoshi	year before last
お腹	おなか	onaka	stomach
同じ	おなじ	onaji	same
お姉さん	おねえさん	oneesan	older sister
お祖母さん	おばあさん	obaasan	grandmother
お風呂	おふろ	ofuro	bath
覚える	おぼえる	oboeru	to remember
面白い	おもしろい	omoshiroi	interesting
泳ぐ	およぐ	oyogu	to swim
降りる	おりる	oriru	to get off
終わる	おわる	owaru	to finish
音楽	おんがく	ongaku	music
外国	がいこく	gaikoku	foreign country
外国人	がいこくじん	gaikokujin	foreigner
会社	かいしゃ	kaisha	company
階段	かいだん	kaidan	stairs
返す	かえす	kaesu	to return something
帰る	かえる	kaeru	to return home
顔	かお	kao	face
かかる		kakaru	to take (time/money)
鍵	かぎ	kagi	key
かける		kakeru	to call (phone)
傘	かさ	kasa	umbrella
家族	かぞく	kazoku	family

方	かた	kata	person (polite)
カップ		kappu	cup
角	かど	kado	corner
鞄	かばん	kaban	bag
花瓶	かびん	kabin	vase
被る	かぶる	kaburu	to wear (hat)
紙	かみ	kami	paper
カメラ		kamera	camera
辛い	からい	karai	spicy
体	からだ	karada	body
軽い	かるい	karui	light (weight)
カレンダー		karendā	calendar
黄色	きいろ	kiiro	yellow
消える	きえる	kieru	to disappear
聞く	きく	kiku	to listen
汚い	きたない	kitanai	dirty
切手	きって	kitte	postage stamp
切符	きっぷ	kippu	ticket
嫌い	きらい	kirai	dislike
着る	きる	kiru	to wear
切る	きる	kiru	to cut
綺麗	きれい	kirei	beautiful, clean
薬	くすり	kusuri	medicine
下さい	ください	kudasai	please
果物	くだもの	kudamono	fruit
靴	くつ	kutsu	shoes
靴下	くつした	kutsushita	socks
曇り	くもり	kumori	cloudy weather
暗い	くらい	kurai	dark
クラス		kurasu	class
グラム		guramu	gram
黒	くろ	kuro	black

今朝	けさ	kesa	this morning
警官	けいかん	keikan	policeman
結婚	けっこん	kekkon	marriage
玄関	げんかん	genkan	entrance
元気	げんき	genki	healthy
交番	こうばん	kōban	police box
声	こえ	koe	voice
コート		kōto	coat
コーヒー		kōhī	coffee
ここ		koko	here
九日	ここのか	kokonoka	ninth day
九つ	ここのつ	kokonotsu	nine things
答える	こたえる	kotaeru	to answer
こちら		kochira	this way
今年	ことし	kotoshi	this year
言葉	ことば	kotoba	word, language
子供	こども	kodomo	child
ご飯	ごはん	gohan	meal, rice
コピー		kopi	copy
困る	こまる	komaru	to be troubled
今月	こんげつ	kongetsu	this month
今週	こんしゅう	konshū	this week
こんな		konna	such
財布	さいふ	saifu	wallet
魚	さかな	sakana	fish
咲く	さく	saku	to bloom
作文	さくぶん	sakubun	composition
寒い	さむい	samui	cold (weather)
再来年	さらいねん	sarainen	year after next
散歩する	さんぽする	sanpo suru	to take a walk
塩	しお	shio	salt
しかし		shikashi	however

時間	じかん	jikan	time
仕事	しごと	shigoto	job
辞書	じしょ	jisho	dictionary
静か	しずか	shizuka	quiet
質問	しつもん	shitsumon	question
自転車	じてんしゃ	jitensha	bicycle
死ぬ	しぬ	shinu	to die
閉まる	しまる	shimaru	to close
閉める	しめる	shimeru	to close
締める	しめる	shimeru	to fasten
写真	しゃしん	shashin	photograph
シャツ		shatsu	shirt
週	しゅう	shū	week
宿題	しゅくだい	shukudai	homework
上手	じょうず	jōzu	skillful
丈夫	じょうぶ	jōbu	healthy, sturdy
食堂	しょくどう	shokudō	cafeteria
知る	しる	shiru	to know
白い	しろい	shiroi	white
新聞	しんぶん	shinbun	newspaper
吸う	すう	suu	to inhale, smoke
好き	すき	suki	like
少ない	すくない	sukunai	few
少し	すこし	sukoshi	a little
涼しい	すずしい	suzushii	cool (weather)
住む	すむ	sumu	to live
座る	すわる	suwaru	to sit
背	せ	se	height, stature
生徒	せいと	seito	student
石鹸	せっけん	sekken	soap
狭い	せまい	semai	narrow
千	せん	sen	thousand

先月	せんげつ	sengetsu	last month
先週	せんしゅう	senshū	last week
洗濯	せんたく	sentaku	laundry
掃除する	そうじする	sōji suru	to clean
外	そと	soto	outside
そば		soba	nearby
空	そら	sora	sky
大学	だいがく	daigaku	university
大使館	たいしかん	taishikan	embassy
大切	たいせつ	taisetsu	important
高い	たかい	takai	high, expensive
たくさん		takusan	many
立つ	たつ	tatsu	to stand
楽しい	たのしい	tanoshii	enjoyable
食べ物	たべもの	tabemono	food
食べる	たべる	taberu	to eat
卵	たまご	tamago	egg
誕生日	たんじょうび	tanjōbi	birthday
近い	ちかい	chikai	near
地下鉄	ちかてつ	chikatetsu	subway
地図	ちず	chizu	map
茶色	ちゃいろ	chairo	brown
一日	ついたち	tsuitachi	first day
使う	つかう	tsukau	to use
疲れる	つかれる	tsukareru	to get tired
次	つぎ	tsugi	next
着く	つく	tsuku	to arrive
机	つくえ	tsukue	desk
作る	つくる	tsukuru	to make
冷たい	つめたい	tsumetai	cold (to touch)
強い	つよい	tsuyoi	strong
手	て	te	hand

出かける	でかける	dekakeru	to go out
出口	でぐち	deguchi	exit
電気	でんき	denki	electricity
電車	でんしゃ	densha	train
戸	と	to	door
動物	どうぶつ	dōbutsu	animal
遠い	とおい	tōi	far
時々	ときどき	tokidoki	sometimes
所	ところ	tokoro	place
図書館	としょかん	toshokan	library
友達	ともだち	tomodachi	friend
鳥	とり	tori	bird
鳥肉	とりにく	toriniku	chicken meat
撮る	とる	toru	to take (photo)
魚	さかな	sakana	fish
七	なな	nana	seven
習う	ならう	narau	to learn
何	なに	nani	what
なる	なる	naru	to become
肉	にく	niku	meat
西	にし	nishi	west
日曜日	にちようび	nichiyōbi	Sunday
荷物	にもつ	nimotsu	luggage
庭	にわ	niwa	garden
脱ぐ	ぬぐ	nugu	to take off clothes
猫	ねこ	neko	cat
寝る	ねる	neru	to sleep
飲み物	のみもの	nomimono	drink
飲む	のむ	nomu	to drink
乗る	のる	noru	to ride
歯	は	ha	tooth
灰皿	はいざら	haizara	ashtray

入る	はいる	hairu	to enter
履く	はく	haku	to wear (shoes)
箱	はこ	hako	box
初めて	はじめて	hajimete	for the first time
始まる	はじまる	hajimaru	to begin
バス		basu	bus
働く	はたらく	hataraku	to work
八	はち	hachi	eight
花	はな	hana	flower
話す	はなす	hanasu	to speak
早い	はやい	hayai	early
春	はる	haru	spring
晴れる	はれる	hareru	to clear up
半	はん	han	half
晩	ばん	ban	evening
番号	ばんごう	bangō	number
晩御飯	ばんごはん	bangohan	dinner
引く	ひく	hiku	to pull
弾く	ひく	hiku	to play (instrument)
低い	ひくい	hikui	low
飛行機	ひこうき	hikōki	airplane
人	ひと	hito	person
一つ	ひとつ	hitotsu	one thing
一人	ひとり	hitori	one person
暇	ひま	hima	free time
病院	びょういん	byōin	hospital
病気	びょうき	byōki	illness
昼	ひる	hiru	noon
昼ご飯	ひるごはん	hirugohan	lunch
封筒	ふうとう	fūtō	envelope
プール		pūru	pool
吹く	ふく	fuku	to blow

服	ふく	fuku	clothes
豚肉	ぶたにく	butaniku	pork
二つ	ふたつ	futatsu	two things
太い	ふとい	futoi	fat
冬	ふゆ	fuyu	winter
降る	ふる	furu	to fall (rain, snow)
古い	ふるい	furui	old
文章	ぶんしょう	bunshō	sentence
下手	へた	heta	unskillful
部屋	へや	heya	room
便利	べんり	benri	convenient
帽子	ぼうし	bōshi	hat
欲しい	ほしい	hoshii	want
細い	ほそい	hosoi	thin
本	ほん	hon	book
毎朝	まいあさ	maiasa	every morning
毎月	まいつき	maitsuki	every month
毎週	まいしゅう	maishū	every week
毎日	まいにち	mainichi	every day
毎年	まいとし	maitoshi	every year
毎晩	まいばん	maiban	every night
町	まち	machi	town
待つ	まつ	matsu	to wait
窓	まど	mado	window
万	まん	man	ten thousand
右	みぎ	migi	right
短い	みじかい	mijikai	short
店	みせ	mise	shop
見せる	みせる	miseru	to show
緑	みどり	midori	green
皆さん	みなさん	minasan	everyone
見る	みる	miru	to see

六日	むいか	muika	sixth day
難しい	むずかしい	muzukashii	difficult
六つ	むっつ	muttsu	six things
村	むら	mura	village
目	め	me	eye
眼鏡	めがね	megane	glasses
もう		mō	already
もう一度	もういちど	mō ichido	once more
木曜日	もくようび	mokuyōbi	Thursday
持つ	もつ	motsu	to hold
物	もの	mono	thing
問題	もんだい	mondai	problem
八百屋	やおや	yaoya	vegetable shop
野菜	やさい	yasai	vegetable
安い	やすい	yasui	cheap
休み	やすみ	yasumi	holiday, rest
休む	やすむ	yasumu	to rest
八つ	やっつ	yattsu	eight things
夕方	ゆうがた	yūgata	evening
夕飯	ゆうはん	yūhan	dinner
有名	ゆうめい	yūmei	famous
雪	ゆき	yuki	snow
行く	いく	iku	to go
洋服	ようふく	yōfuku	Western clothes
良く	よく	yoku	often
横	よこ	yoko	side
呼ぶ	よぶ	yobu	to call
読む	よむ	yomu	to read
夜	よる	yoru	night
来月	らいげつ	raigetsu	next month
来週	らいしゅう	raishū	next week
来年	らいねん	rainen	next year

旅行	りょこう	ryokō	travel
零	れい	rei	zero
練習する	れんしゅうする	renshū suru	to practice
分かる	わかる	wakaru	to understand
忘れる	わすれる	wasureru	to forget
私	わたし	watashi	I
渡す	わたす	watasu	to hand over
渡る	わたる	wataru	to cross
悪い	わるい	warui	bad

Note: Some words do not have kanji commonly used at the N5 level and are written in hiragana or katakana

Afterword

Thank you for joining me on this journey through Japanese Reading Practice for Beginners: 60 Guided Stories. Writing this book was a project filled with a deep appreciation for the learning process, and I hope it has offered you not only valuable practice but also a growing connection to Japanese language and culture. Each story, line-by-line breakdown, and vocabulary explanation was crafted to make learning Japanese as inviting and accessible as possible. I hope that, through these pages, you felt encouraged, challenged, and rewarded as you progressed.

Learning a language is more than mastering grammar and vocabulary; it's about opening yourself up to new perspectives and insights that can broaden your view of the world. Each sentence you read, each kanji you practiced, and each comprehension question you answered brought you closer to understanding Japanese not just as a language but as a means of connection. With every story, you've learned something more about the rhythm of Japanese life, the subtle nuances of its expressions, and the beauty of its simplicity.

As you complete this book, I hope you take away not just the skills you've gained, but a sense of accomplishment and confidence. You've taken a significant step toward fluency and have built a foundation that will serve you well on your continued journey. I encourage you to keep reading, keep practicing, and keep exploring Japanese—there's so much more to discover. Whether you choose to dive into more advanced reading, practice conversational skills, or travel to Japan one day, remember that each step you take is part of a lifelong learning process that you can enjoy at your own pace.

Thank you once again for allowing this book to be a part of your language-learning journey. I hope it's been a valuable companion, and that you look back on these stories with pride and fondness. May your curiosity and love for learning continue to grow, and may Japanese bring you as much joy and connection as it has brought me.

With warmest wishes,
Haruki Yamamoto

Made in the USA
Columbia, SC
06 January 2025

51275530R00154